Getting I.T. Right

Praise for *Getting I.T. Right*

An overall great read for not only executives, but IT project managers, IT staff as a whole, and business units requesting projects. All would benefit from this. Perfect for organizations initiating a PMO as it provides insight into what is to come and, most importantly, what is expected from the various stakeholders. **It helped me organize my thinking so I could help my team.**

—Suzan Abdurrahman, PMP

This book is **a good reminder of the things to consider when managing a new technology deployment**.

—Gary Swick, President, Swick Technologies

If you are anticipating some type of technological change, update, or installation at your company, you better order this book right away. Dr. Jim Bohn, the Blue Collar Scholar, has hit **just the right combination of strategy and "how to"** in his third book, *Getting I.T. Right: A Leader's Guide for Successfully Installing the Organizational "App."* His **insights and practical advice will save you thousands if not millions of dollars, along with keeping your team on task and not heading for the door.**

—Wayne Breitbarth, author of *The Power Formula for LinkedIn Success: Kick-Start Your Business, Brand and Job Search*

For many people in corporate leadership, rolling out a new technology platform brings to mind ugly four-letter words. That's normally because no one has ever shown them **the road map to successful implementation.** Typically, the decision to roll out a new app is made on high, forced downward throughout the rest of the organization by a PM as quickly and "cost-effectively" as possible. In reality, this is the slowest and most expensive path that can be chosen. You need a more **holistic and inclusive approach that spans all stakeholders** to be successful. **This book will teach you specific actionable steps that can be used to make sure your sizable investment in a new technology platform produces positive results.**

—Patrick Torhorst, Chief Information Officer, Quest CE

Jim Bohn has a **no-nonsense, common-sense approach** to breaking down problems. He uses his **lifetime of experience to help organizations prepare themselves for the challenges and changes they will face** as they implement major IT projects.

—Doug Riegle, Regal Ware

In *Getting I.T. Right*, Jim Bohn reveals **a crisp road map that ensures the successful introduction of new information technology into organizations of all sizes.** He presents the seven key principles necessary for an effective new technology launch and **nails the "how-to" of a new system roll out.** His emphasis on change management and communication strategies alone make this book a must-read for executive leaders and IT project managers alike.

—Stephen G. Smith, President & CEO
BrightFlare Performance Solutions

One of the most painful—and potentially lucrative—transformations an organization can undertake is to implement new technology. In my role, I cannot tell you the number of technology "improvements" I have seen devastate a company, creating problems that could have been avoided with sound leadership. I have personally witnessed both the 95% of the implementations that failed, and the 5% that succeeded. Jim's latest book is leading us to be in the 5%, step by step, struggle by struggle. His **unique combination of storytelling and intellectual reasoning both engages and challenges us as we learn.** Re-introducing us to Torva Karachenko and her latest challenges at the fictional Catalyst Medical Systems to serve as our eyes and ears through their arduous journey, **Jim helps us understand what sound leadership looks like, both in best practices and the human part off the equation.** The result is a combination of business principles and real-world challenges that guide us through the pitfalls and the successes that can follow. Congratulations, Jim, another home run!

—Patrick Riley, President and CEO
Riley Technologies dba New Horizons of Wisconsin

Getting I.T. Right
A Leader's Guide for Effectively Installing the Organizational "App"

by Jim Bohn, PhD

ProAxios Publications

JIM BOHN holds a doctorate in Leadership from the University of Wisconsin–Milwaukee and is the author of research on organizational transformation published in multiple journals. A regular lecturer at the University of Wisconsin-Milwaukee, Concordia University, and Marquette University, his previous books include *Architects of Change: Practical Tools for Executives to Build, Lead and Sustain Organizational Initiatives*, *The Nuts and Bolts of Leadership*. *Fixing A Broken Team*, *Improving Management Effectiveness Through ProAction*, and *The Art and Science of Middle Management*.

Getting I.T. Right
A Leaders' Guide for Effectively Installing the Organizational App

Copyright © 2017 by Jim Bohn
All rights reserved.

ProAxios Publications
855 Ulao Road
Grafton, WI 53024

Editing and interior design by Laurel A. Kashinn, WriteStuffResources.com

Publication Date: October, 2017

Printed by CreateSpace

ISBN-13: 978-1545358658

ISBN-10: 1545358656

Table of Contents

Dedication ix
Foreword..xi
Acknowledgments...xii
Introduction
        Headquarters Conference Room, Monday, 8:00 am 1
        Why read this book?
        A brief note on brevity
        How leaders can benefit from this book
        Wanted: clarity in planning for new enterprise apps
Part I.   **Seven Principles for Effectively Introducing Technology**............... 7
Part II. **Risks in Installing the Organizational App** 29
        Sixteen System Installation Risks to Manage
Part III. **A Case Study in Installing the Organizational App** 37
        Goals Checklist
        Case Study: Catalyst Medical Systems
        Executives' Role: Analyze and Lead
Part IV: **Nuts & Bolts of Installing the Organizational App**
        Change Management 57
        Form the Executive Team
        Develop the Rationale for Change
        Select the Project Leader
        Due Diligence and Assessment Reporting
        Define the Change Scope and Metrics
        Select CORE Change Team Leadership
        Select CORE Change Team Members
        Establish governance relationship with Vendor
        Assess Organizational Impact · People
        Assess Organizational Impact · Systems & Data
        Select Field Team Members
        Prepare Communication Plan
        Prepare Testing Plan
        Prepare Training Plan
        Prepare and Deploy Go-Live Support
Part V. **Troubleshooting** 79
        Eight Common Project Crises and Solutions
Appendices 81
        Special Technology Communication Issues, 81
        Timeline, 87
        Terms, 93
        Technical Articles, 95
        Business Network Design & OSI, 97
        Notes / Selected Bibliography, 99
        About the Author, 101

Dedication

One would imagine that a book with significant technical information would be dedicated to a professor of engineering or software technology. This book is dedicated to those in the K-12 teaching profession who instilled in me a powerful thirst for learning:

My second-grade teacher, Miss Gallagher, who had high levels of enthusiasm for history and geography—and Irish dancing. My fifth-grade teacher, Mrs. Hanson, who demonstrated care and compassion to a student under obvious domestic distress, and whose marvelous SRA reading packets challenged my abilities. My sixth-grade teacher, Miss Samm, who had the foresight to allow students to stage their own version of "A Christmas Carol," allowing creativity to enter learning. She understood the extreme power of autonomous motivation. There were others—high school teachers who challenged an obviously capable and clearly distracted teenager —and brought me into the wider world of Steinbeck, Hemingway, Sinclair, Poe, Twain and London, American authors I still read to this day. Mr. Johnson, who let me read the biography of Vladimir Lenin in eighth grade, instilling a deep interest in history and political movements. Mr. Vils, who gave me the opportunity to speak my mind at the high school graduation, which was followed by a standing ovation, launching a belief I could do more if I chose to do so.

K-12 teachers rarely get their due praise, so I offer mine now. Those listed—and more whose names I can no longer remember—were deeply influential in developing a young man who still finds learning as food for the soul.

I am in their debt. They put up with a rebellious, troubled child, and poured in the life-giving fuel of learning and the infinite wellspring of intrinsic motivation that continues to pull me forward. Their influence is incredible and I am grateful.

To them I dedicate this book.

Jim Bohn, PhD.
The Blue Collar Scholar
www.proaxios.com

Foreword

Information technology projects have cemented themselves as the twenty-first century equivalent of building the Colosseum: they are grand and bold, filling the dreams of executives with promises of revenue and efficiency. But the path to the opening games is inevitably fraught with planned and unplanned change. Much of this is because, sadly, companies often overlook the level of effort and detail required for success before embarking.

The discipline of change management is regularly chided by the rank and file as being arbitrary and contrived. Jumping through the hoops, getting the message out, endless meetings and change reviews—in the midst of this, the change control process can feel like a weighty, near-pointless endeavor. Though veteran leaders sense intuitively the fundamental reasons why control processes exist, even the most capable can lose sight of the core of what makes an IT project great.

In *Getting I.T. Right*, Jim Bohn finds the spirit of delivering world-class IT project execution, distills it, and provides it to the reader in a way that is universally sensible and uplifting. A seasoned manager whose decades of experience have seen technology projects begin and end under an array of auspices, he brings a level of credibility to the subject which few can compare. It is this precise credibility, refined in the crucible of research, which slams home so effectively a subject that is growing in demand with each passing day for all senior IT leaders and project managers.

—Jeremy Jones
CIO, Comfort Systems USA

Acknowledgments

A book is a team sport. While the author may have some concepts and ideas in mind, it takes many people to bring a book to life. Foremost, my thanks to Laurel Kashinn for taking a messy manuscript and providing significant professional polish!

My learning in this subject came through the hard work of installing the organizational app. I want to thank Jim Hanson, Chuck Forsyth, strong leaders who led some dramatic projects, for demonstrating the leadership required to get things done. In addition, I think of many team members I worked with on several large IT projects during my career. Dave Mercier's persistence was an immense help in bringing systems to life. Likewise I owe thanks to Mary Cunningham, an exceptionally sharp manager who sought out the details to ensure we had a good solution. Mark Nolan was a finance person who could explain systems with exceptional clarity. Laura Mitchell was an inspiring IT leader and working with her was a lot of fun!

The many fine IT people I worked with also deserve praise for their dedication to process and explanations of things foreign to me, like interface and coding. Although their knowledge was far superior to mine, I always felt they wanted to teach and help me and others as we fought through long hours and tough decisions.

Head and shoulders above the rest, however, were Michael and Brigida Shertzer, the most amazing of the bunch, exceptionally patient and thoughtful and above all, brilliant. To work with them was pure joy in a world of complexity.

I would also like to thank these readers for filling in the gaps I may have missed or for challenging my thinking in specific areas. In some cases I completely missed critical elements which my readers have brought to my attention. Each of them has different levels of expertise, either in large scale project management, executive expertise, technical expertise, systems analysis expertise and business process expertise. There is no doubt in my mind that they know much more than I do in their domains, and thus I asked for their input along the way. I am grateful for the richness of insight and valuable suggestions of Suzan Abdurrahman, Doug Reigle, Jim Smith, Wayne Breithbarth, John Juds, Jason Juds, Mike Sekula, Jeremy Jones, Erica Tetuan, Stephen Smith, Patrick Riley, Patrick Torhorst, and Gary Swick.

Each one has made this book a better work product because of their varied experience, intellectual power, and wisdom. Many thanks to all for helping other leaders in the future, as the pace of IT change accelerates around the world.

Jim Bohn, 2017

Introduction

Headquarters Conference Room
Monday, 8:00 a.m.

Downcast, sallow faces. Dark circles under bloodshot eyes. Slouched shoulders, frowns, and furrowed brows. Every one of the 20-person project team shares the look: exhaustion, frustration, depression. Some stare with clenched jaws and fists. Others sink in their chairs, eyes closed, dozing, or praying they won't soon be out on the street. All are long-past ready to throw in the towel. But that option is only a dream.

A $10-million-dollar project has ballooned into a $30-million-dollar project. Request after request for more funding ensues as a 9-month implementation has morphed beyond twenty four. Impacted are employees, factories, suppliers, and customers. Legal disputes fester between client and consultant questioning who is responsible for disastrous results: inaccurate data, whole sections of financial statements missing, a new system far slower than the old one. Field reps and remote technicians struggle to answer frantic customer calls and provide service, unable to quickly access required information in the new system.

The entire company in disarray.

Today is the day to bring the project status to upper management. Again.

Upper management team members file in. Questions fly. Answers and data are presented. Leaders rub their heads in frustration. Many fidget in their chairs. Others lean towards their project leaders. More agonizing questions, with more unacceptable answers. Faces go red.

But there is no way out. The project simply has to be completed. The consultants, meanwhile, sit quietly, listening with stone faces, perhaps hiding secret eagerness for the inevitable cue: sink more time and more money into the project. There is no turning back now. Too much is at stake both in terms of leadership ego and "sunk cost." They know it. Everyone knows it.

So much could be improved. So much pain and stress could be avoided—if only leaders could have honestly and fully assessed what they were getting themselves into. If only they had prepared, effectively, to install the 'organizational app.'

That is what this book is about.

Why read this book?

People jokingly quip "there's an app for that." Yet organizations have "apps," enterprise applications that are critically important to make them competitive, financially successful, and to change organizational culture. However, introducing new applications creates immense stress from top to bottom. Everyone is affected. Technology introductions require a clear path to success, but the path is overgrown, if it even exists. Teams never quite get good at system introductions because they do them so sporadically. Team members change, technologies change, and applications change, with little to no learning or continuity from one project to the next. Lessons from past projects are often lost.

Organizations spend millions and expend the priceless resource of human motivation installing new applications. Large projects more often than not go off track, taking twice the time and three times the budget to complete, diluting the presumed return on investment. Only 25 percent of corporations report sustaining long-term gains made from change initiatives, according to a Towers-Watson survey.[1] The costs are immense.

This book provides leaders with the precise gritty details of how to introduce new technology and guide organizations to succeed at installing the organizational app.

Although consultants may be aware of some details in this book, they may not always share them. Sometimes that happens deliberately to increase billing. Sometimes withholding information provides a way to blame a client for not having their act together. Often, however, consultants just don't know all these details, nor have the staff to manage them. As a leader, you cannot risk trusting everything to a consultant.

Your payoff for taking the time to read, understand, and apply this book

If you've been called upon to lead a major IT project of installing the organizational app, you have a unique opportunity in your career. Accomplish one of these monsters and your work will become a thing of corporate legend. Fail to do so through ineffective due diligence, excessive scope, a failed relationship with your consultant, or underestimating your own time investment—and your work will become a monument of a different kind.

Think about it.

A brief note on brevity

The executives I have worked with over a lifetime prefer 'the bottom line.' Chief executives, project leaders, directors, and managers are all extremely busy and require cut-to-the-chase answers. Thus, this guide has been tightly edited for maximum effectiveness. Several chapters are quite short and 'to-the-point.' This book is less talk and more action. Executives appreciate that.

How Leaders Can Benefit from this Book

Getting I.T. Right is an invaluable guidebook that provides leaders with a clear and comprehensive blueprint to achieve success, whether the project is monster sized or smaller. Filled with relevant examples, important questions, and crucial checklists, the book is an essential roadmap through the complexities of organizational change, from initial planning through collaboration with consultants to choosing and managing teams.

When companies elect to change IT infrastructure, it is often a headache for everybody. The functioning of the organization from the executive suite to shipping and receiving is often affected. Obtaining buy-in by all stakeholders can be nearly impossible. This book offers massive headache relief by helping everyone prepare to be prepared for change.

"Senior managers have likely never opened up an enterprise resource planning system in their lives," said Mike Sekula, Vice-President of INPRO. Yet senior executives tend to add technology to their organizations at an alarming rate, whether in the on-going search for the next productivity push, provide a customer-satisfaction boost, or to improve financials. Frequently, they do not know what they are getting themselves into. Until now.

Getting I.T. Right: A Leader's Handbook for Effectively Introducing the Organizational "App" provides a roadmap for successfully introducing new technology into organizations large and small, providing precisely what is needed:

(1) A clear set of fundamental principles to guide the project
(2) Sixteen critical risks to be managed
(3) An instructive case study for those new to IT introductions
(4) A series of specific, actionable steps to take

"One of the benefits of this book is it helps an organization come to terms with the changes and challenges they will face," said Doug Reigle of Regalware. "Senior management can begin to help their organization understand what the challenges will be, and more importantly, avoid many of the pitfalls that happen during an IT project implementation. It helped me to organize my thinking so that I could help my team as they deal with the challenges and changes to come."

Wanted: Clarity in planning for new enterprise apps

"What is the one thing you don't want to hear from your chief information officer?" asked the Wall Street Journal of Bernard Tyson, Chairman and CEO of Kaiser-Permanente.

"How great everything is going to be," he answered. "There is a low tolerance for BS, right? ... It's hell, right? It's changing the world."

The second thing he doesn't want to hear:

"It's only going to cost X amount'. It never costs only X amount.

"Third, I don't need a CIO to tell me: 'just implement the technology and you will force the transformation of the organization.' We've experienced that and just the opposite happened."[2]

Sometime in recent months, you and your executive team or organization decided to make a dramatic change in your organization. You are going to implement a new IT System. It could be an ERP, LMS, HRM, CRM, and on and on. The alphabet soup of technology is endless, and it's likely to get more complex in the years ahead. Organizations will continue to change and technology will be at the heart of organization-wide improvement. Big data, IoT and other looming strategic concepts will force organizations to continually add/change/revise the organizational DNA called Information Technology.

Deloitte Consulting published a white paper entitled *ERP's Second Wave: Maximizing the value of ERP-enabled processes.* In their *Top Ten Findings of ERP's Second Wave*, they noted:

An ERP implementation is, at its core, a people project. As respondents make clear, the biggest challenge before and after implementation is not technology – only 19 percent of respondents cite technology as the prime challenge in the post-implementation period. Rather, 51 percent of the respondents said the biggest issues are people related. Respondents made it equally clear that at every stage, companies must work harder still to manage change, secure buy-in, communicate with and educate their employees. Top human resource issues in the survey: change management, training, and internal staff adequacy.[3]

That was in 1998.

Decades later, system-wide technology changes continue to cause exceptionally complex organizational changes—and suffer abysmally low success rates. In a 2013 post-change survey of 276 medium to large corporations by Tower-Watsons, only 55 percent reported achieving short-term initiatives, with only 25 percent achieving their long term goals.[4] That is a full 75-percent failure rate—primarily because organizations fail to develop expertise in leadership of implementing them. The list of multiple ERP and other technology failures is long. See Appendix C on page 95 for a few of the most instructive.

With so many years of technology introductions, it would seem we should have enough information to forge a clear path to technology implementation success. But we do not.

So what's the missing piece when installing the organizational app?

What's missing is a fundamental, philosophical, thorough, and multifaceted understanding of what organizations are getting themselves into when they launch an ERP or other technology introduction, along with set of concrete steps and actions that can be built into a project plan. Such understanding and steps can radically improve the effectiveness of technology projects—which is what this book is about. Developed through experience with multiple technology introductions in a large, Fortune 100 organization, and projects within other Fortune 500 organizations, this book collects together the wisdom and learning that leaders on the ground, on the job, need. This book is about understanding and managing organizational impact.

Based on my experience with significantly large IT projects, this book is an inventory of all that is required to effectively launch new technology. This book is not just about technology, it's also about the people impact and the teams of teams who are involved.

Consider the following graphic.

INSTALLING THE ORGANIZATIONAL APP IS A BIGGER DEAL THAN YOU THINK!

Effective Leaders Consider all the Groups and Interactions Required to Fully Achieve Effective IT Change

ORGANIZATIONAL IMPACT of IT CHANGE

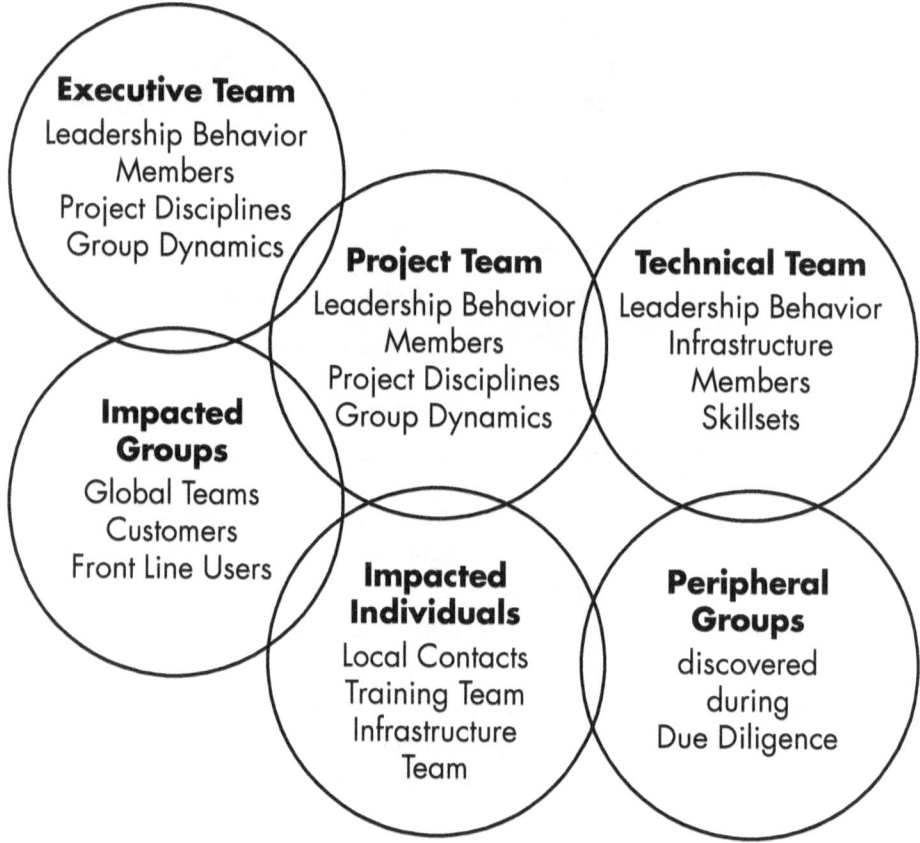

Each group has its own challenges, responsibilities, and commitments to make if the organization is to achieve ROI.

Throughout this book, I lay out the specific details required to ensure all of these groups work together effectively, both in their own teams and with each other.

Part I.
Seven Key Principles for Effectively Introducing Technology in Your Organization

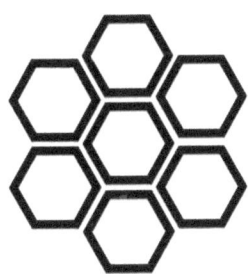

Executives and all members of the project team are to review the following key principles prior to the start of the project: People, ROI Blindness, Due Diligence, Consultants, Participation, Scope, and Leadership. These principles provide insight and form the foundation for how to think about the project. Too often, organizations simply launch into deep water without considering the bigger picture. These principles will ground your project.

PEOPLE
Technology is ultimately about improving the organization to benefit people.

Keep sight of this most critical principle of all: the goal of any technology introduction is to improve the lives of people in the organization, in the contect of company objectives, whether proximally or distally, internally or externally, now or in the future. Improving an organization is a strategic objective, part of which occurs through the introduction of technological solutions. Introducing technology, however, upsets many an apple cart, and the phrase "just do it" doesn't do it.

People's lives will be changed. They will need to exert more energy—at least in the beginning. They will be called on to ADD to their workloads because they will lose team members who are going to become part of a project team. Teams will be under stress, deadlines, budget constraints, and executive demands which come from board-of-director-level demands for accountability on how money is being spent. People will feel incompetent for a while with the new system. They will need good training and support to ensure they 'got it'. They will likely need new equipment. They will need local support to answer questions. They will need to know if the system was effective.

"Re-engineering, therefore, makes enormous demands on managers and their skills. Cost cutting and head chopping is the very easy part of the exercise. The difficult part is to change the company forever. And change of that order is a human, not technical, endeavor."[5]

Executives lose touch with reality when they think their new technology simply will be installed without any impact to their people, and ultimately to their organization. The technology issues discussed in this book support this critical principle. However, this first principle must be kept in mind throughout the project. Tools in a toolbox mean nothing without a good user. Technology is a toolbox, which requires users if it is to be a valuable addition to an organization.

What is the organizational context of this change? People require a satisfying answer to that question.

In addition, people need Leaders to help them with change, which is detailed in Principle #7.

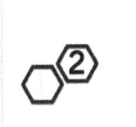

ROI Blindness

Don't let optimism, a.k.a. ROI Blindness, cause you to underestimate the effort required.

"Never, never, never believe any war will be smooth and easy, or that anyone who embarks on the strange voyage can measure the tides and hurricanes he will encounter. The statesman who yields to war fever must realize that once the signal is given, he is no longer the master of policy but the slave of unforeseeable and uncontrollable events."
~Sir Winston Churchill

While Sir Winston Churchill was referring to war, his warnings of becoming "the slave of unforeseeable and uncontrollable events" are accurate for IT projects. Change failure in technology is legendary, as is the volume of articles that follow IT failure. I am convinced most organizations fail to conduct postmortems of projects to determine the roots of failure. This is a huge mistake. Most IT projects are viewed as beneficial to the organization and likely to succeed. Optimism is fueled by a belief that profit is just around the corner. Yet, a major source of failure is often overlooked. Executives, overwhelmed with stars and dollar signs in their eyes—what I call ROI blindness—neglect answering the one question that will make the project a success:

"What are we getting ourselves into?"

Leaders often overlook a serious commitment to diagnosis, including diagnosis of:
(1) the magnitude of the change
(2) expectations of what the change will bring about
(3) systems linking to a primary system (system integrations) and
(4) the pain of the 'societal' or human aspects of the project.

The magnitude of the change includes all of the 'billiard ball effects' to other systems and people. There is often a stark contrast between what consultants say will be in place versus what truly happens when the new technology is in place.

For example, linking the new system to other existing systems is a mind-bending effort requiring serious, in-depth study of the current systems that will 'talk' to the new system. The societal impact of the change takes the greatest toll on organizational resources and can affect hundreds, if not thousands of people who are familiar with a certain way of working and must change how they do things. This is not an insignificant effort.

The benefits of technology introductions? A central system brings together the component parts of our complex organizations and can teach us how the pieces fit together. In the long run, that knowledge can help an organization do amazing things! But don't be fooled - it's going to take a lot of hard work.

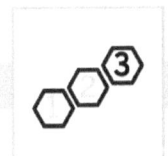

Due Diligence
Prevent unintended consequences.

Understand the complete definition of *Due Diligence*:

1) A measure of prudence, responsibility, and diligence that is expected from, and ordinarily exercised by, a reasonable and prudent person under the circumstances.

2) Duty of a firm's directors and officers to act prudently in evaluating associated risks in all transactions,

3) Duty of the investor to gather necessary information on actual or potential risks involved in an investment

4) Duty of each party to a negotiation to confirm each other's expectations and understandings, and to independently verify the abilities of the other to fulfill the conditions and requirement of the agreement.

Leaders must practice Due Diligence across all areas. Yet for the sake of expedience, leaders often neglect serious Due Diligence when planning to introduce a new system, specifically Due Diligence to assess how the new will interact with old, existing systems. This impacts everyone's daily work to a greater or lesser extent, depending on the role.

Here's the point: Lurking in the background of every IT/System project are unforeseen consequences that occur by tampering with the heart of an organization. Many of those unforeseen consequences happen because of system interfaces. Where the new meets the old.

Here's an example that sounds simple

Suppose you want to automate a current process that uses a manual system to fill orders. A client orders something on the web and they expect to get it shipped to them. Now suppose you want to change that system. Sounds simple, right?

Once a decision is made to move forward, people flock to a meeting where carefully crafted and graphically gorgeous PowerPoint slides show how the new process will work. Heads nod in agreement. More slides show the dramatic improvement the new system will provide. Heads nod with greater energy. Here is the beginning of ROI Blindness, as clearly the Return on Investment looks very strong. Leaders nod with approval. The project is launched with great aplomb. The energy and enthusiasm are contagious...at least at first. Without Due Diligence of System Interfaces, the project is at risk.

Here's the caution

Without effective Due Diligence, the clock is ticking on an unintended discovery of an undiagnosed system interface that will likely bring the project to a grinding halt. It's not complicated. It just takes hard work to discover what you need to know to be successful. That hard work includes getting an inventory of all systems that will be affected by the new processes and tools.

To guide your Due Diligence, here are a few simple outcome questions (as opposed to geek speak)

Note: Answer all in detail!

Need a model? Think of the old SIPOC diagram:

Supplier–Input–Process–Output–Customer

1. Who uses the current system?
2. Who supports the system?
3. Who feeds data to the system?
4. Monthly reporting: who receives data from the system? What are the historical reporting requirements? Who gets reports from the system? (Stop the reports for a while, and see if anyone yells!)
5. How old is the existing system? And will it be replaced? By what?
6. Are there data feeds specifically designed to have an old system talk to a new system? (Note: These are often so deeply hidden no one can find them until the systems don't 'talk.' Very likely, they were built by someone who retired in 1980.)

The answers to these questions will provide you with a strong starting point and a gut check about the complexity of the project. You need to know these details to ensure you budget effectively both in terms of funds and human effort.

Common reasons why organizations don't take time to do *effective* Due Diligence

Generally, by the time the project is being presented to the organization, commitments to savings (in the next year? quarter? month?) have been made. Those commitments have been registered, documented, and remembered by a savvy finance person. The enthusiasm to get going outweighs the boring effort required to dig deep into the inner workings of the current system. Novelty will always win over tedium. Count on it.

"We know enough. ... Let's get started." Details are overlooked because of expediency.

It is best to address Due Diligence as a stand-alone process. While it *can* be done in parallel with other system analysis, doing so is risky, since discovery of old interfaces will likely cause re-thinking of and re-design of existing and new processes.

Pay me now, or pay me later. Truer words were never spoken.

As a leader, you cannot afford to overlook the key activity of Due Diligence in your project. In the end, proper Due Diligence can save tens of thousands, even millions of dollars, as you implement your new system. Find a software engineer who loves the details. Treat them well. Feed them well. Care for them. And tell them to go find every mystery interface lurking in the background.

You will be glad you did.

Consultants

Know how to work with IT consultants.

IT introductions are major investments in time, dollars, human energy, and business opportunity costs (the things you can't do while you're doing something else). These investments in technology often impact mission-critical systems that form the DNA of the organization: data repositories, systems for order management and fulfillment, customer contact systems, and telephony and internet interfaces. Clearly these projects have dramatic impact on organizational performance. Given the major challenges of these IT introductions, organizations often use external consultants to advise and provide everything from project management to change management. External consultants have the expertise and they can staff up or down, depending on the needs of the project.

A few considerations

IT consultants are not part of your organization—and that is a triple-edged sword.

(1) They will take up much time learning what your organization does and that translates into US$, CAN$, Euros, Pounds, Yen.... Name your currency.

(2) Not being part of your organization allows them to push and say things internal people may not feel comfortable addressing. That's a good thing, and a key lever to use during organizational change.

(3) IT consultants, however, will not be working for your organization after the project is done, at least not for a while. They are not as invested in the outcome as you are. They can leave; you remain. During the sales

process, IT consultants are likely to provide a glamorous view of projected savings, improved revenues, employee satisfaction, and myriad other benefits. This is normal and natural; however, their projections may be unrealistic. I have not seen companies check out the BEFORE and AFTER effects of an IT implementation, comparing initial projections with actuals. You may want to consider that in your assessment, and especially in your contract.

Finally, most IT projects run over on time and cost: it's a fact of organizational life. When push comes to shove—and it often does—IT consultants will want to cut time to reduce cost. That's not a bad idea; however, it can cause problems if they cut critical process analysis steps. I've seen it and it isn't pretty.

For payment, set milestones. Make payments contingent upon successful conversion with client data, instead of paying up front.

When consultants cut corners, you may not like the results

Organizations don't undergo massive IT projects every day. Thus they need the assistance of IT consultants who can manage the details.

A bit of caution is in order. Take the time to understand and develop the relationship you have with the consultant, set careful boundaries and expectations, especially in areas like process mapping and technical documentation. After all, they are working for you!

Consultants, of course, can be extremely helpful. Just understand their limits and set your own expectations for their performance.

Participation

Organizational participation: the impact of IT Projects on "day jobs."

A system introduction places heavy demands on company-wide resources. People have 'day jobs.' Consequently, team leaders must understand who are the team members and what their concerns are, from their point of view.

To adopt the correct point of view and understand this principle, let's shift perspective now, and step into the shoes of those on the ground:

We work in finance, procurement, sales, human resources, and operations, among other roles. When a major IT System change comes into our organization, sometimes we're asked to join a team to help implement the new System. From a Change Management perspective, that's a great idea because it is critical to engage multiple stakeholders in the process to ensure a complete implementation. Organizational participation is critical to success, and we are on board.

Let's go back to our day job for a moment. Our finance, procurement, sales, human resources and operations roles do not prepare us for the grueling details of IT/System implementation. Even the savviest among us may find ourselves bewildered by the project. IT/System projects are weird around the edges and use language we don't understand. In short, these projects are not what we were hired to do.

A few reasons why we struggle when asked to join large IT projects

1. We are brought together around levels of complexity that may boggle the mind! And what about our 'day job?' Although we're often flattered and intrigued by being selected to support the project, we have concerns about our current job.

2. We've been asked to commit hours, days, maybe weeks and months to the project. We have other priorities to manage.
3. We've heard a project like this has been attempted before...and failed.
4. We don't want to have our careers tarnished by failure or waste our time on something that won't increase our personal value.
5. We've heard we must travel, adding further complexity to an already busy schedule.

We need to manage the risk in our participation

We are exposed to a brand-new language. There are new terms we need to learn. So what can we do to be successful when invited to participate?

Participation Tips for Our Team Leaders

1. **Leaders**: work with our teams to delegate responsibilities to open up the bandwidth for your participation in the project.

2. **Gain a clear picture of our involvement**: what are the expectations for time, effort, project deliverables?

3. **Ask for clarity on our level of influence**: Do we have the right to question process or protocol when it seems like things are not moving in a good direction? What do we do when that happens?

4. **Learn the terminology, as painful as that may be**. Meetings are difficult. Meetings with non-stop misunderstood complex technical terms are impossible.

5. **You and I have a day job**. Our organization wants us to invest very heavily in a new system to improve performance. It's to our benefit and the benefit of others to improve, so get on board and help us help the effort. Just take the time to ask some questions early in the process, to understand what you're getting into.

Scope

Manage Scope!

Occasionally, the film industry will produce a comedy about something that starts small and turns into a nightmare. If they did a film about an IT systems project, it would probably best fit in the category of science fiction, because ineffective management of scope can grow to other-worldly proportions. There are many terms for this, most notably "scope creep"— which is an interesting double entendre, don't you think? Beware! There are *scope creeps* in your company!

Managing scope is notoriously challenging!

Scope Challenge #1: Let's fix what we've never fixed!

When word gets out that a new system is being implemented, managers often see a way to resolve chronic issues that have plagued the organization for months, years, or even decades. It sounds like this: "Well, as long as we're doing ABC, let's add XYZ."

While scope is generally established at the beginning of a project, odd things appear during Due Diligence—which is why to conduct Due Diligence well in advance of project start up. The whereabouts of Jimmy Hoffa, an infamous American union boss, was in the news as of this writing because of the mysteries surrounding his death. There is an analogy here for IT/Systems projects: some hidden system will present itself—at the wrong time—causing scope creep.

Although people start with a clear view of scope, it is inevitable that new discoveries will cause change and additions, typically in terms of system interfaces developed long ago.

Scope Challenge #2: Beware the Infiltrators

Another subtle reason scope is increased is a form of sabotage. Those who are truly opposed to the project will give the appearance of interest and participation while adding layers of demanding complexity, that will ultimately subvert and sabotage success. Then they'll say "I told you this wouldn't work."

Scope Challenge #3: Adding complexity—don't do it!

When you add more software and more capability to a system, you make things more complex. Walk before you run. Always strive for simplicity. One system at a time, not time cards and health care and human resource management, etc.

Too much complexity is a recipe for frustration and failure!

What to do when people want to add scope

We all learned when we were 2 years old a very powerful word: "No." Why not use that as a lever? Have the person who wants to add scope articulate the impact to the project, in terms of dollars, human cost, opportunity cost, project delays, and additional consulting fees. While they may have a valid reason for adding scope (improved ROI) it's a really good idea to get a sharp understanding of what the addition means, and that they're committed beyond their criticism.

Determine in advance who has the authority to say "no," and make sure everyone on the team knows who it is and why. Is it the project manager? If not, then saying "no" needs to come from an executive level as well.

Stay alert!

Be wary of someone who says you're not a team player if you won't add scope. It takes managerial discipline and courage to set very hard boundaries around a project—and it is one of the best ways to ensure project success, to finish on time and within budget.

Leaders Help People Change
Help your people adjust to change.

To help the people in your organization be successful at navigating through the changes, get on board with the changes, and even assist in the changes you want to make, take time to understand the following five principles. Consider this seventh Key Principle a starting point for further reading and discovery about human behavior.

Most important: Leaders must make make every effort to:

1. **Reduce Anxiety:** Reducing anxiety increases adaption. Accept that people are emotional beings and strive to sooth feelings and reduce anxiety.
2. **Simplify:** Understand that people learn best in small bits.
3. **Follow Through:** Know that follow-through is the path to accountability.
4. **Measure for Course Correction and Celebration:** Recognize that people like to see the progress of measurement, and understand why.
5. **Build Trust:** Know that people will either gain or lose trust with each new change.

---

1. Reduce anxiety to increase adaptation.

Adventurous, novelty-seeking souls who enjoy constant change are rare. Most people are wary of the 'new.' In business, 'new' is often costly in terms of personal effort, time, money, and even physical discomfort; have you ever had to move your desk from one building to another? The new is uncertain, and as research by Robert Snyder reveals:

> "High levels of uncertainty and ambiguity are typically inherent in large-scale organizational changes and are close correlates of resistance to change." [6]

Additional research by James Allen concurs:

> "Within the context of organizational change, research has demonstrated that uncertainty is often a major consequence for

employees…in relation to a range of different organizational issues, including the rationale behind the change, the process of implementation, and the expected outcomes of the change. Consequently, organizational change is a major stressor during which employees seek to gain some prediction and understanding over events to minimize their uncertainty." [7]

How does reducing anxiety increase adaptation?

Anxiety is not a normal state. Anxiety is the result of resistance. If my mind is not clouded by, say, whether I'll have a job when the change is done, or whether this change is going to completely upset my apple cart, or if it is going to cause me to look incompetent, or if it will put me into a team with a bunch of people I have never worked with—or worse, with people I don't want to work with—my anxiety will be reduced.

The reverse is also true. Keep me in the dark about the change and I promise to be ineffective during a time a great stress. In fact, I may even resist the change to protect my own interests. The greater the unknown, the higher the anxiety and the lower the adaptation.

Resistance to change is based in neurology

NEWS FLASH: The human brain is wired to conserve energy, and new things cause the brain to expend a great deal of energy. With cognitive energy expenditure comes anxiety ... and with anxiety comes resistance.

There is no one "cookie cutter" solution. Here are suggestions to reduce anxiety. (Hint: great leaders do these things regularly.)

1. Start thinking about what would reduce team member anxiety. What will reduce apprehension and concern?

2. Effective communication is essential to reduction in anxiety. The operative word: 'effective,' not excessive!

3. Be straight with people. HINT: Lies do NOT help, nor do half-truths. If you can't tell people something, let them know that.

4. Bring clarity to the change which allows people to sort out what it will mean to their lives.

5. Regular updates help. People will make conclusions about things they do not understand.

6. Model the change, don't just talk about it.

Leaders: Think about your people.
What would reduce anxiety during change?

Reduce anxiety, increase adaptation. If you want change to 'take hold' in the DNA of your organization, this action is not optional. It doesn't mean people won't have concerns about the change. It just means they will increase their trust in your leadership, and that bodes well for the long-term success of your organization.

---

2. Simplify to increase adoption.

In watering a garden, which way is better for saturating the soil and for the health of the plants?

A) Set the hose to a soft sprinkle and deliver the water to gently and slowly to fully saturate the soil, in small drops

B) Deliver the water in a concentrated blasting stream like a fire hose

I shall never forget a meeting I participated in as a sales executive, newly promoted into a sales role. We were greeted on a Monday morning by several cheerful vice presidents. They explained that we would be receiving 'training' that week. What followed was nothing short of amazing. For eight to nine hours per day, every day that week, we were subjected to a tag-team line up of the finest PowerPoint jockeys in the world, talking about every product, process, and service we could possibly sell.

By Friday night that week, had you looked me in the eye and asked "what did you learn?" I honestly could not have said more than "there's a lot of stuff to learn." To say I was exhausted, and not much smarter, would be an understatement. And I was a whole lot wiser from the experience.

HINT: A key leader in the training world likes to say "TELLING AIN'T TRAINING."

Sadly, I have witnessed many "fire hose" training events like this over the years. Developed by well-intended, efficiency-minded individuals, I would wager they never had to sit through a session like that. Learning theory and practice offers a different approach.

If you want people to absorb, learn, and retain the information they learn, **distributed practice** is the key.

Distributed practice is best way to train

"Massed practice"—the story of my firehose-like sales training experience—is the approach used quite often in corporations. The gentle sprinkle opposite is called "distributed practice."

Research shows that the smaller intense cloudbursts of training and learning called "distributive practice" are far superior to long, drenching sessions that exhaust and drain the mind rather than fill it.

Simplify to increase adoption

Implications: When we're managing change, we need to provide people with enough knowledge to become competent without overwhelming them. The good new is, in an age of online learning, Distributed Practice is eminently possible with any audience.

Not only that, give them smaller bytes, and they will love you for it.

What else do we need to do to simplify?

In any change, people can drown in a tidal wave of information. They will become fearful that they cannot absorb everything they need to know, and very often, they will become exhausted.

Smaller, more compact and clear segments in shorter bursts will improve adoption rates.

Change is not easy. Complex change is hard. Offering people systematic segments of carefully planned learning is a key element of making planting, growing, and watering the new change to be a vital part of your organization.

Summary: To increase adoption, simplify

3. Follow-through to increase integration.

In tennis, golf, baseball, fly fishing, and just about any sport requiring a fluid motion to achieve a goal, you hear the phrase "follow-through." I love baseball, so I'll use that sport in my analogy.

It's a simple thought, really. You have an intended action (hit a home run), you make a preparatory motion (pick up the bat), you conduct a primary motion— "Swing batter, batter, batter"—and then you follow-through. The only time a batter doesn't follow-through is when they intentionally restrain the effort to avoid a 'strike.' But no one hits a home run when they check their swing. It ain't happenin.' The follow-through is just as important to the motion of swinging for the fences as any other part of the activity...

Why would we miss the follow-through in Change Management? Why check the swing?

Reasons why managers *must* follow through

Follow-through in change management is the most boring of the principles. However, it is, in my opinion, the most critical.

1. People want to know if you're serious about this change. Follow-through demonstrates commitment.
2. People have a lot on their plates, and it's easy to forget the new change. Follow-through helps them to remember.
3. People sometimes resist change because it is costly. Follow-through shows you are not changing the change. It is going to happen.
4. People sometimes simply need reminders amidst distraction.

We all know the importance of 'sticking with something'

We've heard it from youth. Follow-through is nothing more (or less!) than persistence. We all know persistence pays.

If the change was worth investing in,
    If the change was worth the human effort,
        If the change will make a difference for your organization,
            If the change has long-term strategic value...

Change doesn't happen without follow-up. It won't become integrated into your organization if you don't persist.

Summary: Follow-through to increase integration!

4. Measure for course correction and celebration.

While we all have opinions about various and sundry things, and in business, medicine, research, education, and science, measurement trumps opinion. And if you don't believe things can be measured, check the tax code: the government can measure anything! Everyone has ideas, thoughts, concepts, and words we use to communicate what we're doing, and most of the time, we accept the progress we see from others. However, **when the time for change comes, we must measure.**

In point of fact, we all have internal systems of measurement we use every day. For example:

"I think I've lost a few pounds."

"Have you noticed how different the downtown area looks?"

"The manufacturer of those jeans seems to have cut back on quality."

We all evaluate things—ranging from the mundane to the critical. It's part of human nature to see how things transform, and we have internal "gut feels" for how things are changing. Thus the need for measurement in change should not surprise us. Yet it often does.

Why measure?

For correction.
For celebration.
For commitment.

Correction - When a change is underway, we need checkpoints along the way to assess whether the change is truly taking hold in our organizations. Clearly, with the heavy investments we make in change, a checkpoint is critical to assess whether we're truly making a difference in the fabric of our organizations, or if we simply appear to do so!

Celebration - Teams work their hearts out when introducing new change. If you measure the impact of the change, you can demonstrate the value of their effort and reward them accordingly. Teams like recognition much better when they can see results. (And so do executives!)

Commitment - When people on the front lines are asked to participate in the evaluating, measuring, and providing feedback, and when their evaluations, measurements, and feedback are heard, acknowledged, valued, and responded to clearly and appropriately, then something magical happens. People put a part of themselves into it, and they become invested in the project.

What reasons do people give to NOT measure?

1. It takes too much time.
2. We don't really have anything we can measure.
3. No one agrees on what to measure.
4. We don't have good data.
5. We don't have a simple system for measurement.

Now think about each one of those excuses—because that's what they are—and ponder this. Don't good managers measure performance? And since they do, they have found ways to assess what's happening with people. Each of those excuses can be answered and resolved.

Reasons why people WILL measure:

1. **This is easy, it only takes moment.** Make the system as simple as possible. See #4.

2. **I see exactly what to measure.** Make it very clear what's being measured or evaluated.

3. **It's very clear and relevant.** Clarify the why: what will happen when we change or improve? What will happen if we don't? How will the new way impact everyone when we do it right? What will happen to everyone if we don't do it right? We need you to help us make sure that it happens right. You are an important and valued contributor to something big, that will help other people. Motivation science tells us that everyone wants to be valued and valuable.

4. **Create transparent feedback loops.** For example, post clipboards at water coolers to solicit feedback, key responses into a database accessible by all to share the data being collected by everyone in real-time. Don't use suggestion boxes or closed systems that anonymize and hide data. When people see others participating, when they can see the ideas their colleagues have, when they later see the ideas turned into data and being used constructively, it will encourage participation.

5. **Make the system as simple as possible!** Enlist the troops in creating the simplest way. People know their work routines; provide them with the opportunity to contribute to how the data is to be collected. People will have good ideas for ways to fit a measurement system into their lives as simply as possible, when they know the goals are simplicity and clarity, understand the relevancy, and feel respected and honored by being part of something bigger than them.

Measure for correction, celebration, and commitment. It's a great way to motivate people and navigate change.

Like I said, if you don't think things can be measured, consider the tax code. If the government can measure anything in order to tax it, surely we can measure things at work in order to improve things for people.

---

5. All change either builds or destroys trust.

This principle may sound stern, perhaps even harsh, but in my experience, it's true.

Think about it for a moment.

At different points in the history of your organizations, you've experienced changes that *built* confidence, and changes that *eroded* confidence in leadership. You have either felt a sense of leadership interest in the welfare of people and the interest of the organization, or you didn't sense it.

Though trust is a delicate thing which is easily broken, it is also a powerful element of influence in organizations.

Think again.

If you sense that someone has your best interest in mind, and you see evidence of care and thoughtfulness, your trust increases. And if you sense something is not right, your trust decreases.

Trust is a motivator like no other. When people trust their leaders during a time of change, they are inclined to add their personal energies to the task. All change demonstrates the level of the organization's interest in the welfare of their employees, even in situations where the change may run counter to employee expectations.

Trust is built through...

1. Clear explanations of the rationale for the change
2. Constant and consistent communication of change progress
3. Training to help employees learn the new process or program
4. Support that helps people when they're challenged because of the change
5. Recognition of the extra effort people put in to make the change happen
6. Removing ineffective team members

Leadership Summary

Keep in mind that these five principles of **how to lead by helping people change** are merely a great starting point for further reading and discovery. What's important is that you take the time to:

(1) Accept as an asset the emotional nature of people: *anxiety* during change is a harsh reality, *enthusiasm* is priceless.

(2) Understand that people learn best in small bits.

(3) Be very aware that follow-through is the path to accountability.

(4) People like to see the progress of measurement.

(5) People gain or lose trust with each new change. Focus on the gain.

The Seven Key Principles Review

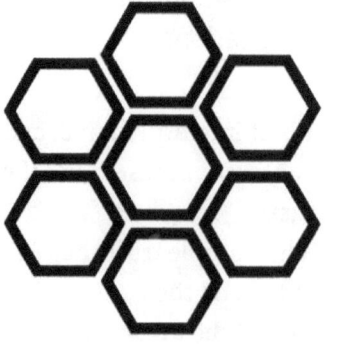

1. People
2. ROI Blindness
3. Due Diligence
4. Consultants
5. Participation
6. Scope
7. Leadership

Part II.

System Rollout Risks When Installing the Organizational App

This section outlines 16 risks inherent in every IT project rollout. Study each risk carefully, keep each in mind throughout the process, and assess whether you, your leadership team, or executives have succumbed to the risk. Review the actions and determine whether you have effectively managed this risk.

RISK 1. ROI Blindness.

Perceived ROI sometimes makes rational people irrational. Rare is the organization that goes back to check the *original* ROI to determine if it achieved the financial benefits it promised. Executives must be brutally honest about the true financial and human toll required. As a leader, you may be infected with this malady. Understand that the PowerPoint slides of consultants are long gone and forgotten once the project picks up speed—and the consultants are gone, too. I often have thought consultants should get their final 1/3 only when the project has demonstrated results. Beware the big numbers consultants sell you. They won't be around to pick up the pieces.

ACTION

Bring data. Ask a lot of questions from the consultant, including references and evidence of past success. Raise issues about participation and effort. Who is doing what? What is the true ROI?

RISK 2. Your organization is not prepared for the change.

The old gospel song asks "Are you ready?" Have you thought through how, where, and when this implementation will affect your organization? Do you have the capacity for this change? In terms of resources, what must be moved or added? Which projects must be put on hold? What are the costs of the opportunity? Have you conducted Organizational Diagnostics in the context of the IT change? In other words, what OTHER projects are happening at the same time? Is your organization ready to work *together* to accomplish this change? Does the organization understand the 'why?' Can the organization 'stay the course?' Are the leaders in place to manage the scope of the change? You must conduct in-depth preparatory analyses of these questions to ensure a comprehensive understanding of all aspects of the IT scope.

ACTION

Answer the questions above. Take the time to effectively evaluate organizational capacity for installing the organizational app.

RISK 3. Using the "B" Team when only the "A" team will do.

Are you fooling yourself into thinking that those with spare time on their hands are the right people for the job, simply because they are available? Think again. B-team members know why they are being selected, and they will mark time until something else comes up. It is tempting to throw B-team members at a project, but it is not wise. Put the B-team players into a maintenance project. Top talent is critical for the success of these projects.

ACTION

Raise the issue. Remind the organization about the long-term impact of the project on funding, productivity, customer satisfaction, employee motivation and project credibility. Parenthetically: Using the A players means you provide them with incentives for being part of this incredibly complex project.

RISK 4. Denying the business impact of installing the organizational app. Some revenue loss will occur.

Research by Gartner and others shows your organization will not perform at the same level during the introduction of a new system. There are revenue and profit implications to adding a new system. What is your plan? Ignoring this issue will not make it go away. Manage it by assessing the risk and developing alternate streams of revenue.

ACTION

Raise the issue. Plan for one division to pull weight to adjust for the change. Make appropriate financial adjustments in advance of the change during the time period in which you will GO LIVE.

RISK 5. The wheels on the bus go round and round.

Your organization needs to continue to serve customers and care for employees during the change. You are changing a tire on a moving vehicle. What are your contingency plans to manage the business while it is moving?

ACTION

TEST, TEST, TEST and TEST again! Ensure a back-up plan is in place during 'GO-LIVE' in case disaster or hiccup so business can resort to the old way momentarily (not permanently) while fixes are put in place.

RISK 6. The Jimmy Hoffa syndrome—where are the bodies buried?

Your system analysts will discover unexpected software patches that must be integrated with the new system, some built in COBOL = $$$$. Uncover those pitfalls early in your due diligence! They are expensive discoveries to make after the fact.

ACTION

Due diligence for all interfaces must be a priority at the very beginning of the project. Ensure someone's feet are held to the fire to do an outstanding job of detective work. This is a non-negotiable element of the project. Put your best people in this role, and have them articulate precisely what the cost will be to integrate the system with these old feeds.

RISK 7. I get by with a little help from my friends.

Installing the organizational app is going to impact a LOT of unforeseen individuals and teams. Discover who will be impacted. Chat around the water cooler and listen. Learn about stakeholders, risks, and other concerns. Make sure communications go out in newsletters and the intranet. The more the word is out there, the more you will find out. I can assure you: The impact matters to those who are impacted! Working with them dramatically increases your chances of a successful launch.

ACTION

Determine all groups that will be impacted – even those on the periphery of the project. This work can be done in concert with the Due Diligence for System Interfaces.

RISK 8. Ado Annie syndrome: SCOPE HAPPENS.

Ado Annie is the character in the musical *Oklahoma* who constantly says: "I can't say 'No.'" Without discipline, projects grow into monstrosities, becoming impossible to implement. Scope happens. Do not allow 'customization' to creep in!

ACTION

Executive leadership sets and **HOLDS** the articulated boundaries of the project, taking responsibility for and backing up those empowered to say "No."

RISK 9. Automating bad processes.

Do not write Technical Design Documents without first having gone through Process ReDesign. Resist this impulse or you will wind up automating a bad process. Process Redesign is arduous, exhausting, painstaking work, and it must be done.

ACTION

Assemble the Process ReDesign team early in the project plan* and ensure a complete set of processes has been analyzed before the tech design documents are written.

RISK 10. Not "counting the cost" of all that it will take to complete the project.

The Biblical adage about ensuring you can finish what you start is wonderful ancient wisdom. Consider the whole cost—people, process, and finances. Are you really determined to complete this project? Do all team members know what it will take, including the business unit requesting the change? Throughout the duration of the project, when team members get overwhelmed, executives must be ready to step in to keep leaders on track to completion.

ACTION

Ask yourself and your executive team if, after assessing all of these risks and doing your due diligence, you are truly committed to getting this thing done.

---

* See Appendix A, **Special Technology Communication Issues,** p. 81, including an ideal Timeline for Installing the Organizational App, pp. 86-87

RISK 11. Ignoring the details.

In global projects, the precise meaning of terms is crucial. For example, in India, "clubbing" means somthing different than in the West. Always define terms. Develop standard revision controls, and agree upon project disciplines. **This is painstaking work that is worth the time and effort.**

ACTION

The details of revision levels, contract agreements, a clear understanding of what a 'change request' means, and on and on. The Devil is truly in these details and they can be exceptionally costly if overlooked.

RISK 12. Be careful not to develop an adversarial relationship with your vendors.

It's easy to fall into this trap, arguing over contract details from the very beginning of the project until the last line of code is completed. This trap causes excessive expenditure of precious energy you need for the implementation of your system.

ACTION

Set the stage up front with clear expectations about how you will work together, who is responsible for what, establishing timelines, costs, and agreements on contact points in the organization. These are all areas where thing can go awry from the outset. Take the time to effectively develop the relationship from the beginning. Once it becomes adversarial, the project is in bigger trouble, because that's when the 'blame game' sets in.

RISK 13. Adequate end-user training.

Ensure adequate end-user training. People cannot function and don't like working in a system they can't understand.

ACTION

Stage end-user training 2 weeks before Go-Live, not any sooner. People like to be trained, and then get to use the system.

RISK 14. Data migration path must be clear.

Transferring of data between systems, is a key consideration.

ACTION

Make sure time is allowed for both automated and manual data cleaning and verification with parallel runs of both systems to identify disparities and prevent loss of data. Make sure time is allowed for multiple passes through verification, as needed.

RISK 15. Review historical information.

What historical information will need to be retained?

ACTION

Review historical information retrieval and recall requirements.

RISK 16. Be aware of infrastructure changes and interfaces.

For example, Android v. iOS iPhone interfaces.

ACTION

Consider and plan for all infrastructure that may be affected by the change.

Review of Installation Risks

1. ROI Blindness.
2. Your organization is not prepared for the change.
3. Using the "B" Team when only the "A" team will do.
4. Denying the business impact of installing the organizational app. Some revenue loss will occur.
5. The wheels on the bus go round and round.
6. The Jimmy Hoffa syndrome—where are the bodies buried?
7. I get by with a little help from my friends.
8. Ado Annie syndrome: SCOPE HAPPENS.
9. Automating bad processes.
10. Not "counting the cost" of all that it will take to complete the project.
11. Ignoring the details.
12. Be careful not to develop an adversarial relationship with your vendors.
13. Adequate end-use training.
14. Data migration path must be clear.
15. Review historical information.
16. Be aware of infrastructure changes and interfaces.

Part III.

A Case Study in System Rollout Management
Complete all sections of this case *with your team.*

Goals Checklist

____ Develop an increased awareness of the complexity of system change through a case-study format. The case study is built from direct experience with multiple changes in Fortune 100 organizations.

____ Assess of your change situation.

____ Develop a workable change-action plan.

____ Understand the things that *can* go wrong, and the things that *must* go right.

Describe your upcoming technology change:

_____
_____
_____
_____
_____
_____
_____

Case Study: Catalyst Medical Systems

Take the time to read through and discuss this case study with all team members and colleagues who have a vested interest in the system outcome and ROI. The 'gotchas' of IT system implementation are embedded in it.

The Team

Individual	Responsibility	Bio
Dr. Miriam Alexander London	CEO – Catalyst Medical Systems	Highly respected researcher, biologist, multiple patented medical devices, expert in pediatric orthopedics.
Jonathan Smith	Vice President of Operations – UK	29-year veteran of medical device industry; served multiple roles in operations, finance, service. Diplomate Engineering.
Tina Vasquez	Global Vice President of Sales	Hired six months ago; strong track record of sales growth in former roles.
Luke Stinson	Project manager from Navigator Software	Hired to promote standardization, financially incented to complete project ahead of schedule.
Andrea Beauchamp	Chief Research Scientist	Hired by Dr. Alexander
William Tenwirth	Finance Executive - CFO	Former Chief Executive of Brewster Medical, acquired by Catalyst last year
Egan Mgebe	Customer Service Manager, Johannesburg	Former Brewster branch office
Customer Service Team in Johannesburg	Support all customer orders, returns, and tech support problems in Africa	21-person call center with multilingual CSRs.
Torva Karachenko	Customer Service Manager - Dallas	Newly transferred from St. Louis, formerly of Brewster Medical
Customer Service Team in Dallas	Support all customer orders, returns, and tech support problems in NA	45-person call center with multilingual CSRs.
Daniel Jackson	Customer Service Rep in Dallas	2-year employee

BACKGROUND

Catalyst Medical Systems

Catalyst was developed in 1992 to provide post-surgical care for complex pediatric joint fractures. The repair of pediatric joint damage is made complex by growth plates which must be properly managed as the joint is healed. Through years of research, Catalyst pioneer Dr. Miriam Alexander developed the technology and was appointed Chief Executive Officer by the Board of Directors in 2010.

Catalyst sales offices are distributed across the globe, serving 27 countries on four continents, including South America, North America, Europe and Africa.

Brewster Medical Devices

This organization competed with Catalyst until last year, when Catalyst Medical Systems acquired them and their advanced technology for pediatric joint replacement. Brewster was headquartered in London, but in 2013 they moved their primary offices to Johannesburg to support the expanding African markets. William Tenwirth had been Chief Executive Officer of Brewster since it's inaugural production in 1975.

DuCharme Industries

DuCharme has rapidly become a major competitor to Catalyst and recently developed a biomedical system that speeds recovery for pediatric patients by 18% over existing methods.

Brewster Medical Devices	Catalyst Medical Systems	DuCharme Industries
1975	1992	2009

The Compelling Event

CEO Dr. Miriam Alexander looked deeply concerned as she stared out the window at the first snow of the new year. Her CFO, William Tenwirth, and her COO, Jonathan Smith, sat across from her. There was light knock as the door opened.

"Good morning, Dr. Alexander," said Tina Vasquez, Global VP of Sales, entering, nodding to her associates, and taking the last free chair.

"Hello Tina," said Dr. Alexander. "Thanks for coming, everyone. Hope you all had a good holiday. Looking through year-end reports, I am concerned. We're down 12% year-over-year. What is the source of this issue? Why are we losing business to our competitors?"

"Our competition argues that Catalyst has no true centralized systems for technical support," Tina responded. "That fact has caused sales losses in several major competitive situations. It's true. When global customers ask us whether we can take calls and support anywhere, the ultimate answer is 'no.'"

"Well, what can be done?" Dr. Alexander asked. A brilliant medical expert, she was not an Operations specialist. "Clearly we're not the only organization that has faced this issue."

"We could install a centralized system for global support," recommended Jonathan Smith, VP Operations. "There are many tools available today. Corporations do this all the time. We simply grew too fast with our acquisitions."

Dr. Alexander turned to her CFO. "William, we have funds in capital planning for this year."

"Yes," he answered abruptly. "I agree, we need a system. In fact, Brewster had an excellent system for tracking and support and parts ordering. I'm not sure why you've never invested in a global system. And, I need to remind you, those funds are for R&D and facility maintenance."

Dr. Alexander was silent in thought for just a moment. "Alright," she said. "I will authorize up to five million pounds to get this moving. We need to get the system in place, now. Jonathan, you have the lead on this. I want regular updates."

As she adjourned the meeting, she turned to Tina Vasquez. "Will this solve the problem we're facing?"

"It will make a major difference," Tina responded. "I will inform my sales team today."

* * * * * * * * * *

What are your personal observations of their change situation?

___

A Leader's Guide for Installing the Organizational App | 43

Jonathan Smith assembled a team of several people in the UK with participation from IT, Sourcing, and Operations. Within three weeks, they had chosen an off-the-shelf package from Navigator Software for logging technical support calls, and hired Luke Stinson from Navigator as the project leader. Navigator is headquartered in the United States.

Individual	What responsibilities does this person own during the upcoming change?	What personal goals does this individual have?
Dr. Miriam Alexander, CEO		
Jonathon Smith, VP of Operations—UK		
Tina Vasquez, VP of Sales		
Luke Stinson, Project Manager from Navigator Software		
William Tenwirth, CFO		

How are their personal goals likely to conflict as the project moves along?

_____

_____

_____

What will galvanize and bring them together?

_____

_____

_____

Group Work

What happens if Catalyst doesn't make this change?

_____
_____
_____
_____

What challenges will this change present to Catalyst Medical Systems?

_____
_____
_____
_____

What organizational tensions will arise as this change proceeds?

_____
_____
_____
_____
_____

How is this leadership team managing this change? What would you recommend to them? What could have been done differently at the start of the project?

_____
_____
_____
_____
_____

London: Life goes on

In the months after her meeting with Dr. Alexander, Tina Vasquez had worked hard to ensure everything was on track, and she remained energized. On the third Monday in July, she typed an e-mail to Andrea Beauchamp, Chief Researcher:

> DuCharme Industries is rapidly gaining ground in Europe and America. We need the new product released immediately. When do you anticipate product launch?

Days went by and Tina had no response from Andrea. On Thursday she walked down the hall and into to her office.

"Did you see my email?" she asked, without knocking at the door.

"Yes, I saw your email," came the quick retort. "We are nearly ready to release the product, but several tests remain. We're working on it."

Tina pressed the issue further. "Are you confident we can outperform DuCharme's product?"

A bit irritated, Andrea did not look up from her computer.

Tina asked again, "Can we outperform DuCharme's product??"

Andrea looked over the top of her glasses, then responded. "These things take time. Products that heal human beings are complicated and complex. We don't turn them out like cardboard cutouts. You sales people are always rushing things."

"But six months ago, you said it would be released by now. We have a major sales challenge. DuCharme is gaining serious market share and we need to have a big splash to show we're competitive. It's important that we meet the deadlines we set. We have customers waiting. We're not meeting our numbers!"

Scowling, Andrea looked back at her screen. "I'll send you an email after I meet with the product team."

Tina walked away, muttering to herself. Later that afternoon she received an email from Andrea Beauchamp:

"The product team says we will likely deliver first versions to the field in the next three weeks. It's a tight schedule, but I have been assured it can be done."

Armed with this new information, Tina arranged a conference call to inform her sales team that the new product was on it's way.

What influence will this pressure add to the systems change that Catalyst is about to undergo?

_____
_____
_____
_____

How much does the product team know about the impending system change?

_____
_____
_____
_____

Is there anyone else who should know this change is going on for the change to be effective?

_____
_____
_____
_____

REFLECTION

As you read through this scenario, what similarities do you see between Catalyst and your change situation?

1.

2.

3.

What will you do to stay the course?

_____
_____
_____

What organizational issues will influence your change?

_____
_____
_____
_____

How do you maintain focus?

_____
_____
_____
_____

A Case Study

Dallas - Field Preparation

Later that week, it was a normal day in Catalyst's Dallas Call Center, with more than 500 inbound calls for orders, tech support, and product returns.

Torva Karachenko returned from lunch to see two new emails in her in-box:

```
From: Tina Vasquez, Global Vice-President - Sales: LONDON.
NEW PRODUCT RELEASE - ANNOUNCEMENT
```

> I take pleasure in announcing that Catalyst will be releasing it's new 'therapeutic web technology' by September 1. Watch for specific sales details. This product will provide significant advantage against our major competitor. Notify all managers and supervisors of the pending release.

```
From: Luke Stinson, Project Leader - Navigator Software.
STANDARD GLOBAL CALL SHARING PLATFORM
```

> Greetings all North American call center team members. Within the next several weeks we will be releasing a new system for technical support calls. Watch for further updates! This system will be used globally in the coming months. I look forward to working with you. Luke Stinson - Project Manager - Navigator Software

Torva read through both emails. *Well I'm glad they're going to release that new product*, she thought. *Our customers have been screaming for it after the marketing campaigns. This new system, though, concerns me. We tried this before at Brewster. It was very painful. What sort of help they will provide? We'll need training. I wonder when it will be released?* Her phone rang.

Individual	What responsibilities does this person own during the upcoming change?
Torva Karachenko, Customer Service Manager, Dallas	

Johannesburg – Global notification

This hiring process has been exhausting, Egan Mgebe thought as he rubbed his eyes. *I never thought we would lose so many people when we were acquired by Catalyst.*

Just before heading home for the evening, he scanned two new emails.

From: Tina Vasquez, Global Vice-President – Sales: LONDON. NEW PRODUCT RELEASE - ANNOUNCEMENT

> I take pleasure in announcing that Catalyst will be releasing it's new 'therapeutic web technology' by September 1. Watch for specific sales details. This product will provide significant advantage against our major competitor. Notify all managers and supervisors of the pending release.

From: Luke Stinson, Project Leader – Navigator Software. STANDARD GLOBAL CALL SHARING PLATFORM

> Greetings all North American call center team members. Within the next several weeks we will be releasing a new system for technical support calls. Watch for further updates! This system will be used globally in the coming months. I look forward to working with you.
> Luke Stinson - Project Manager - Navigator Software

"Looks like the American call center has some changes coming it's way," Egan said to his assistant who was also leaving for the day, and shut down his computer.

Individual	What responsibilities does this person own during the upcoming change?
Egan Mgebe, Customer Service Manager, Johannesburg	

Checking in...

Based on the data presented so far, what challenges do you foresee?

1. From a project management (nuts and bolts) perspective ...

2. From a change management (people) perspective

3. From a leadership communications perspective

4. From a coordination perspective

5. From a collaboration perspective

REFLECTION

As you read through this scenario, what similarities
to your change situation do you see?

1.

2.

3.

Change in Progress

Circle (the tensions you see) in the Catalyst scenario below.

Sao Paulo – Customer issues

Delays in the system launch to different parts of the world prevented global customers from getting global service.

Surgeons at the Hospital Brigadeiro São Paulo SP contacted the Dallas Help Desk. A traffic accident involving a school bus on the Rodovia Adhemar de Barros has caused multiple injuries to 17 grade-school children. The orthopedic surgeons had decided to use Catalyst as their supplier for joint healing.

They discovered some technical challenges with the methodology, and with such a large group of injuries, they need immediate assistance.

Dallas

A phone call came in from Sao Paulo requesting assistance on the new product.

Daniel Jackson sat at his desk, staring at the computer screen. The new system had come on line that morning, and he was confused by what he saw.

I'll never be able to do this, he thought to himself. *It's too hard, too complicated.*

Although he had been trained for several hours, the new system was overwhelming. *I'm going to look really stupid to these other reps; I can't even open a customer ticket.*

Torva Karachenko walked by his desk, as he muttered under his breath.

"Everything okay, Daniel?" she asked.

Daniel gasped. "Things used to be a lot easier around here."

"What seems to be the trouble?" Torva asked, a bit concerned.

"I cannot get this system to work, no matter how hard I try," he responded. "I simply cannot access the data I need."

Torva was professional, and hid her own concerns. "Did the training help?" she asked.

"Yes, somewhat, but it was a lot of detail packed into just a few hours. There is no way I can remember all the steps. This system is SO different from the one we used before. Everything is in the wrong place!"

"Well, do the best you can today. I'll get another rep to go over the training with you after your shift."

Torva returned to her desk frustrated and angry. *Does anyone know what's happening here?* she thought. *Those leaders in London completely missed the boat on this. They've failed and now we have to work it out.*

She rapidly emailed Luke Stinson, and copied the Jonathan Smith, VP.

From: Torva Karachenko, Customer Service Manager - Dallas
STANDARD GLOBAL CALL SHARING PLATFORM
To: Luke Stinson, Project Leader - Navigator

> Dear Luke, I'm not sure how you plan to manage the support we're receiving over here in Dallas, but my reps are very concerned about how the system works.

Luke Stinson's reply came within minutes:

> Well, all your people were trained. The system is operating the way it should. I don't understand your concern.

Torva shot back another reply:

> I don't think you understand. We are having trouble supporting customer orders!!!! I don't know what those people in London are doing.

With the following response from Luke Stinson:

> Well, it's really not my problem, I have other things to manage here. They were trained, and as leaders, you have to take charge of the change. If you want, we have another training session for Europe happening at 3 AM your time tomorrow.

Johannesburg

The former Brewster employees in Johannesburg were alarmed and concerned. With all that was involved in the acquisition, they were buried in new paperwork, training, and other organizational changes.

The call centre in Johannesburg buzzed like a hornet's nest with incoming calls for service. The therapeutic technology from Catalyst had a major flaw, and hospitals across Africa were struggling with the new design. Surgeons wanted answers—now.

Egan Mgebe struggled to get his head above water through the barrage of phone calls. He was confused about the latest system changes, though he had been notified several weeks earlier.

"I thought this would be a software patch like we did at the old company. I had no idea it would require a full system upgrade."

Egan heard the complaints of many of his reps.

"You're right," he said to his team. "In my old company, we wouldn't have had a system like this. Everything worked perfectly, and we didn't have ongoing problems. Those people in London have no idea what they're doing."

Egan pitched in to help with the technical issues, listening to calls and helping as much as he could. The team faced a few long days and worked the weekend, finally getting through the challenge.

On Monday, Egan called HQ in London. He was unable to reach Jonathan Smith – so he left a voicemail.

"Why did we implement this new system?" he said. "It's terrible! All my reps can't stand it either. And I agree with them. In my old company we had much better tools. You people at Catalyst have no idea how to support and serve customers, and you have no idea what's going on out in the field. You're all going to destroy our customer relationships!"

A few hours later Jonathan Smith sent an email.

```
Hello Egan - I received your voice mail. We are
working around the clock to resolve the interface
issues. You can check out our website for Frequently
Asked Questions. We are updating them every day. Kind
regards, Jonathan Smith
```

Egan read the email, grimaced and felt his ears grow warm. *Why did we make this change!??*

Executives' Role:
Leading System Change
ANALYZING THE CATALYST SCENARIO

Research indicates that top management support is essential for success, regardless of the type of system. The results of this study are in line with prior research, but with an interesting twist – that the importance of commitment increases over time.[8] —Brown, Chervany and Reinecke

Look for elements in the case study similar to your change. What will you do?

1. The general disruption to the 'system' whenever we engage in a change requires concentration and attention to detail. What will you do?

2. We're all in this together – finger pointing solves nothing. What will you do?

A Leader's Guide for Installing the Organizational App | 55

3. It takes leadership effort, not just words, to coordinate activities. What will you do?

4. Constant communication and follow-up are critical during change. What will you do?

A Case Study

5. Unforeseen circumstances will arise requiring rapid leadership support. What will you do?

6. Executive example is critical – Leadership example matters to everyone. What will you do?

Part IV.

The Nuts & Bolts of How to Install the Organizational App

An Organization is Ready to Deploy the App when:

____ (1) The organization is emotionally prepared for the change and technically trained to execute the business.

____ (2) The organization is technically prepared to execute all customer interactions.

____ (3) Management organization (up to and including executive levels) can effectively manage the business.

____ (4) Data viability for all affected systems has been confirmed.

____ (5) The organization is able to conduct all standard operations reviews.

____ (6) A post-deployment plan is established (new hires, training program, current employees struggling with tool) with enough support staff to answer questions the day the question is asked.

____ (7) Interoperability with other teams (systems, equipment, factory, agents) has been confirmed.

I. Form the Executive Team

Nothing is more critical than ensuring a strong leadership team from the very beginning of the project, who understand the change, who are on board with the change, who support the change, who are committed to the change and who understand the gravity of what is about to take place.

This team will...

1. Develop the rationale for the project.
2. Guide the project from beginning to end. (See Timeline, page 86.)
3. Be available for communication events at the start, during the project, and for recognition at the end.
4. Support the project team with funding, decision-making, guidance, and support.
5. Break down barriers.
6. Manage project team disruptions.
7. Review and engage in the contract negotiations with the vendor.
8. Manage scope!

Notes

II. Develop the Rationale for Change

The leadership team gathers together for as long as it takes to describe carefully, clearly, and cogently: "Here is why we're introducing this technology."

1. What is the organizational context of this change? WHY ARE WE DOING THIS?
2. Clearly define the purpose of the change for the operator on the shop floor!
3. Confirm executive support for rationale – in other words, are all the leaders on the same page?
4. Socialize change rationale with management to ensure understanding and buy in.
5. Remove "Corporate Speak."
6. Provide a clear, concise, compelling answer to the why question that can be stated in less than 60 seconds.
7. Estimated time-line of delivery. Months? Years?

Here are some reasons for technology change, based on discussions with many participants: home-grown system is out of date; old ways of doing things are not effective; changing culture; breaking old habits; impact to business; culture of silos; multiple geographic locations.

Notes

_____
_____
_____
_____
_____
_____

Nuts & Bolts

When developing the rationale, eliminate "Corporate Speak" such as: new functionality; aging software; user experience; automation; performance improvement; business is changing; data visibility; corporate growth; communication. (See page 85.)

III. Select the project leader

This choice will likely influence 75% of project success. The project leader for this type of change is a special breed.

Characteristics of an effective Technology System Project Leader

One frequently overlooked element of effective IT projects is the leader. Organizations often defer to a CIO or some technical genius, but as with all things change, technology is only a part of what is required to ensure your ROI when introducing new technology.

Here are some characteristics I have observed in the best and most successful IT project leaders. Ignore them at your peril.

Suggested Qualifications

1. **Experienced with large scale changes, not necessarily IT, but quantifiable experience with changes.**

    This individual must have several massive organizational changes under their belt. They need to be able to anticipate --- and prevent --- disaster. The organization must acknowledge their expertise in getting things done.

2. **Able to select and bring together an effective team.**

    This individual has the savvy to find the right people necessary who will work together to navigate one of these treacherous journeys. This individual leads the entire team, including the project manager, communications leaders, and more.

3. **Respected by executive management.**

    Though this individual may not be an executive, this leader has the respect and affirmation of upper management and is well known in their ranks. He or she has a known reputation for success and achievement.

4. **Track record of accomplishments with groups that do not report to him or her.**

    This individual has the ability to persuade those who do not report to him or her. They have the logical skills of argument and data management that will win the hearts and minds of others whose skills are needed to get the job done.

5. **Known for persistence.**
   At an almost physical level of hardiness, this person is known for his or her ability to grind out hard projects to the end without wavering. They do not give up when the going gets tough.

6. **Clear-headed under pressure.**
   A sense of being dispassionate and capable of seeing 'the forest for the trees' distinguishes this person. This person is someone who does not easily get riled by the stress.

7. **Effectively communicates with all levels of the organization from the Board of Directors to frontline workers.**
   Someone who can only communicate with senior executives will not win the minds of the rank and file. Conversely, one who is buddy-buddy with everyone will not win the respect of executives. This is a seasoned individual who can communicate across all chains of command and still command respect.

8. **Ability to stay focused on the objective.**
   A leader who gets lost in the details will lose sight of the goal. A leader who gets bogged down in unnecessary details (all details are critical, but not all are equal in weight) will lose sight of the goal. The leader of these projects must keep the end goal in mind and continually remind the team where they are going. It also means the leader must crack the whip on the right occasions - sparingly, but deliberately when needed.

9. **Manages scope.**
   Like wrangling a tiger, the project leader will ensure the project does not get out of control and become more of a monster than intended. Scope creep turns many well designed projects into out-of-control monsters.

10. **Able to bring bad news.**
    Perhaps the most difficult aspect of this role is the ability and requisite courage to diplomatically bring bad news when costs run over or an obscure discovery is made which adds months to the project launch.

11. **Knows Technology itself is not the end goal.**
    While technical knowledge is important, you'll note technical expertise is not even on this list. Here's why. Knowing too much about the technology often drags the leader deep into the guts of the project, instead of maintaining oversight.

Notes

IV. Due Diligence and Assessment of Reporting

Assessing whether the business is running effectively is essential after the technology is in place.

1. Ensure business can be effectively conducted after the change.
2. What financial metrics are mandatory?
3. What reports are essential to management?
4. Confirm data accuracy in reporting during pilot testing.
5. Confirm reporting with stakeholders.
6. What is the follow-up review/postmortem plan at the end?

Notes

V. Define the Change Scope and Metrics

The leadership team gathers together for as long as it takes to carefully, clearly and cogently **define the boundaries of the change and 5-6 metrics that will assess the effectiveness of the change.**

1. Provide clarity on the boundaries of the change including a precise definition of what will and will not change
2. Establish Change Metrics – how will the change effectiveness be measured?
3. Clear definition of metrics – what does each metric mean?
4. Data Access for the metrics – how will data be retrieved?
5. Reporting schedule of the metrics – what is the schedule and who does the reporting?
6. What is the impact of the metrics? What do they mean to the business?

Notes

VI. Select CORE Change Team Leadership.

These members will lead the project for the entire duration of the project.

The leadership team gathers together to select the correct team members who will start and complete the project. Moving tam members in an out during a major project is a recipe for an incomplete job.

1. CORE Team leadership/sponsorship – who owns the change from beginning to end?
2. Program Management Leadership and clarity of responsibilities.
3. Communications Leadership – responsible for all communications analysis, scheduling, conference calls, messaging, socialization of messaging, calendar.
4. What are the precise expectations of team members? Do they retain their existing jobs as well?
5. What additional recognition or compensation will they receive?

   REMINDER: Do not use the "B" team when the "A" team is necessary. "A" players know the business, and become ambassadors for the change. The organization won't respect the solution if made by "B" players.

Notes

VII. Select CORE Change Team Members (duration of project)

These members are part of the project from beginning to end, and are selected as required to represent key groups within the company. Recommended reading: *The Five Dysfunctions of a Team* by Patrick Lencioni.

1. IT
2. HR
3. Finance
4. Legal
5. Data management
6. Other critical teams
7. Field/Factory Subject Matter Experts
8. What are the precise expectations of team members? Do they retain their existing jobs as well?
9. What is the expected meeting cadence? (How often will they meet to review and update the project?)

Notes

_____

_____

_____

_____

_____

_____

_____

_____

_____

_____

_____

VIII. Establish governance relationship with vendor

The vendor(s) relationship(s) have an extreme impact on the project. Clarity must be established upfront to ensure a proper understanding of how the supplier and organization will work together.

1. Expectations of contractual deliverables, including timing and outputs.
2. Role of vendor with respect to Program Director.
3. Boundaries of the change, access to staff and decision making.
4. Build in a drop-dead date; no pay for incomplete work.
5. Set escalation procedures, define exactly what steps to take.
6. Use social media.
7. Find user groups.

Common Vendor Issues you will likely face and must manage:

Recommending development of unnecessary things
No training plan
No detailed documentation
Lack of timely support
Programmers overseas in different time zones
Expenses you didn't know about
Updating systems without informing you
Third-party-integrator blame game
Big Pond – Small Fish syndrome (See Terms, page 93)
What happens if the software doesn't do what it's supposed to do?

Notes

IX. Assess Organizational Impact: People

What are the high-level likely impacts when the new system is in full production across the enterprise? What will be different? This information will provide you with details for your communication plan.

1. Discover the concerns people may have, using structured interviews to get to the root of the most serious issues which need to be addressed.
2. What risks does the change represent? Workload, Leadership, Support?
3. How does the business continue to run during the change? What is the contingency plan?
4. What additional people are needed to complete the work?
5. What is the impact to schedules? Vacations? Work teams? Reporting structure?

Notes

X. Assess Organizational Impact: Systems and Data

What systems will be affected by the introduction of the technology? Who owns all details associated with old and new data? Develop a complete inventory of the systems that are affected. Who is responsible for all data processes, analysis and quality?

1. Data management from old to new systems?
2. Data cleansing – who cleans it up? What are the parameters and business rules?
3. Data transfer – who moves the data from one system to another?
4. Data validation – who ensures the data transferred effectively?
5. System interface inventory – who assesses, defines, and documents this and communicates it to the team?
6. System infrastructure changes requested (See Diagram Appendix D)

Notes

XI. Select Field Team Members (non-central off-site locations)

These members are the local experts who will coordinate with headquarters on all communication, training, development and field interactions, including GO-LIVE logistics.

1. Local "Captain" – responsible for implementation, communication, liaison with corporate team. Manages local logistics (vacation, schedule during GO-LIVE).

2. Has direct contact with the primary (central) project team on a cadence of communication.

3. Establish financial or other incentives for project completion.

Notes

XII. Prepare Communication Plan

A <u>thorough</u> and <u>complete</u> communication plan is essential to the effectiveness of the change. Integrate it with your MASTER PROJECT PLAN.

1. Develop stakeholder assessment – who is affected?
2. Develop key messages by stakeholder.
3. Develop MASTER communications calendar/schedule.
4. Prepare feedback loop/manage rumor control.
5. Prepare FAQs, Conference Calls, Weekly Updates.
6. Define common terminology.
7. Prepare local communication path with local "Captain" with occasional support communications from executives
8. Schedule updates.

Things people expect from a communication plan:
> Why are we doing it?
> When will it happen?
> How does it impact me?
> Will I still have a job?
> Why is this good for the company?
> What if the implementation fails?
> Who do I go to with questions?
> What's the time commitment?
> Where's the money coming from?
> What is the timing?
> What is the scope? Which facilities? Which groups/departments are affected?
> What is happening?
> Who is impacted?
> When will it happen?
> Will I have access to the old system?
> How will status be communicated?
> Will I have to change how I do my job?
> Groups affected: Engineering; Mfg.; Sales; HR; IT; Supply Chain; Warehouse; Inventory; Finance; Field Operations

Notes

XIII. Execute the communications plan—CRITICAL

The plan must be carried out systematically, deliberately, always checking for organizational comprehension to assess whether the communication is getting through.

1. Ensure stakeholders and executives are kept in the loop
2. Respond quickly to issues
3. Address project issues directly
4. Establish framework of 'phasing communication'
5. How will the organization know what is happening?
6. What is the priority of this project compared to others?
7. Develop a feedback mechanism to assess effectiveness.
   <u>Is the communication getting through</u>? <u>How do you know</u>?

Notes

XIV. Prepare Testing Plan (technical team responsibility)

A complete and thorough testing plan must be designed and implemented to ensure GO-LIVE success.

1. Write scripts against business processes
2. Determine test participants
3. Schedules
4. Output details
5. Job coverage during testing
6. Bug fixes
7. Specific test data, know the results in advance to verify the system is working: what I think is going to happen actually happens
8. Daily feed from the existing system
9. Confirm and verify data validation

Notes

XV. Prepare Training Plan

A complete and thorough training plan must be designed and implemented to ensure GO-LIVE success. Training is key to organizational success. It requires deliberate and careful analysis and effective implementation – must be integrated into the Master Project Plan.

1. Select training Owner who is responsible for the entire program.
2. Assess an inventory of Audiences.
3. Categorically understand the system changes that have taken place so the training is focused on what is truly necessary.
4. Develop training materials.
5. Select trainers of high caliber who understand adult learning.
6. Ensure field support during training.
7. Establish training matrix (what is being taught to whom, and when?)
8. Process work instructions.
9. Training schedule: tie training to job flow and current business processes; sales, repairs, etc. Think it out in advance of training.
10. Plan for travel; logistics; time zone issues.
11. Plan for job coverage during training for those who are learning.
12. Additional training resources; computers; internet access.
13. Train-the-trainer sessions.
14. Blackout dates: no one is on vacation, all hands on deck.

Notes

Notes

XVI. Prepare & deploy GO-LIVE support

GOLIVE support is often overlooked due to the exhaustion of resources and project extensions. But GO-LIVE support is critical for success.

1. Who is the Program Manager for deployment to the field?
2. Who owns support?
3. Who supports the field 24X7 during deployment?
4. Who supports the field during GO–LIVE?
5. How do questions get answered? In what time frame?
6. 1-800 line
7. Who are the power users, ie. pilot group of initial testers?
8. Who provides online help to global teams?
9. Who does 'fixes'?
10. Who escalates issues?
11. Deploy a formal process for managing changes to the system.

Notes

Notes

Part V.

Troubleshooting: When the Crisis Hits

Every IT project has crisis moments–they occur naturally as an outcome of project complexity. I've seen several common crises in large projects. Very often these crises begin at the beginning, for without an effective plan things fall apart quickly. Many of these crises are interrelated and often compound one another, but they can be averted by following the actions listed in Part IV.

The key in a crisis is to do a quick analysis of what is happening, make a correction, and move forward. Leadership is required to manage through the crisis. Dragging your feet does not help any project. Keep people moving toward success—don't let them get bogged down in despair.

Common project crises

1. **Vendor relations** – This crisis happens because of poor upfront negotiation about boundaries and expectations. Regroup with the vendor and reset the baseline.

2. **Budget failure** – This happens because executives have underestimated the true cost of implementation and scope creep. Accept the mistake and regroup.

3. **Loss of key personnel** – This happens because team members no longer wish to work on the project and either leave the team or the organization. Regroup quickly and get a strong, solid replacement.

4. **Team failure** – This failure can take several forms, ranging from bad group dynamics (too much tension in the team) to frustration among team members because the right people are not on the team and the team cannot move forward. Sometimes you need to remove a team member who is causing trouble. Have the team leader do a quick analysis and determine next steps. Support the leader!

5. **Data** – Sometimes people miss critical data at the beginning or the data isn't clean, or the data was discovered too late in the project and it has caused a disaster. Make adjustments and move on. Do business process to data mapping at the beginning of a project.

6. **Consensus** – Too much or too little consensus generally happens around processes that will be chosen to do future work. Executive leadership must regroup the team and keep them focused on the end goal and project milestones.

7. **System failure** – When systems fail, the team must discover the reason as quickly as possible, while going back to the old way for only a brief period of time. Know your backout plan up front.

8. **Schedule failure** – Schedules fail because of poor project management. Discover the root cause of the failure (not enough manpower loading? Faulty expectations for technology) and move forward.

There are other reasons for IT project crises, but you get the idea. The key is to resolve the issue as quickly as possible and get the team back on track.

APPENDIX A

Special Technology Communication Issues During Organizational App Installations, with Timeline

I strongly suggest the executive team review this material early in the project to gain an overview of the magnitude of communication needed during technology change. Technology adds a level of complexity to communication. Not everyone needs to know everything that's happening.

Here are the **desired outcomes** of effective communication during system introductions:

1. People understand the change.
2. People gain an understanding of what's happening during the change.
3. They learn how to adapt to the change.
4. They prepare for the change.
5. They integrate the change into day-to-day operations.

Technology Changes place a heavy demand on human attention spans

Technology introductions often encompass tens of thousands (millions) of interconnecting parts, including a significant (Radical?!) amount of detail with terms that are often understood only by specialists.

The Boredom Problem

A Primary Challenge of Communications During an IT project ...

Complexity

+ **Cognitive Demand X** (busy-ness + distraction)

BOREDOM

Boredom is costly in many ways.

The costs of boredom include: time wasted in meetings of unnecessary complexity, opportunity costs (I could be working on something else), lost energy, frustration, leaving people with a sense of: "This is a waste of time!"

IT changes require

significant communication to be effective

... and ...

IT Technology people are experts in IT.

They are generally not trained in communications.

IT people look at

extreme detail and communicate with logic.

Excessive detail they provide can lead to team frustration.

HINT!

High-level summary

at the beginning of meetings.

Stick around if you

want more detail.

Stakeholder Communication During Technology Change

Communication of the technical pieces of technology can be a burden to the team if not properly managed. The key is to ensure the necessary communication is put forth, but the technical elements are reserved only for those who truly need to know – this is to prevent wasted time in meetings and to preserve human energy. These are major categories of communication, which still require significant details as listed above. These categories are presented to give managers and leaders a high-level overview of the major areas which must be covered during a technology change. The high level categories include, PROCESS, DATA, LOGISTICS, TRAINING and INFRASTRUCTURE.

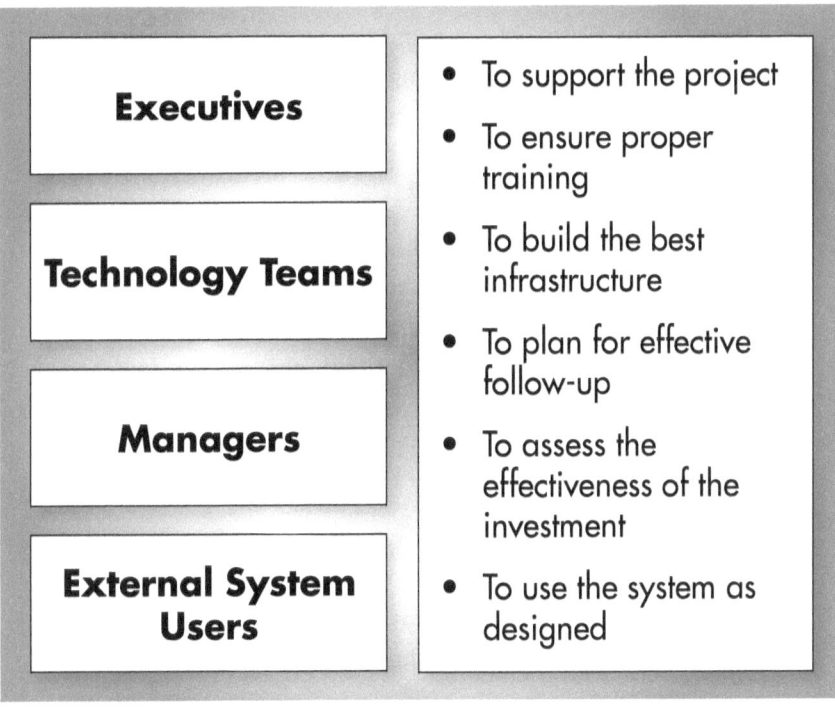

Figure 1.

The groups of people who must be engaged in the communication process. Each Group must receive effective communications in effective formats and language. Not everyone needs to know everything about the technology piece. The reasons for communication are shown in the right column.

Executives

Executive leadership (the leadership team defined above) must be on the same page, literally and figuratively. That 'page' includes timing and a clear understanding of resources required. It also includes costs of installation, vendor issues which must be escalated, and any barriers which impede project progress.

Technology Teams

All of those who are involved directly in the technology piece of the project need to know timing, sharing timing, and provide feedback loops to those who are using the system.

This includes the IT project team and the supporting IT teams who are developing code or working with a supplier or vendor, in addition to those managing infrastructure and hardware.

Managers (Directors) – Middle Level

Anyone in Middle Management who is supporting staff or training people or answering questions must know what is required without getting into the heavy technical details. This key group of leaders needs to know the things that impact their people, how to get answers when trouble strikes, the details and logistics of the 'launch/ GO LIVE", and where to get support for their people.

External System Users

Anyone who is going to use the system to support customers or other internal organizational groups needs clear communication which is not encumbered with technical complexity.

How to Simplify Communications

Format communications by asking (and answering) direct questions that do NOT require technical language.

Approach communications from the standpoint of the listener, not the technology team.

Provide a process checklist. Make it easer for each user to understand the impact to their lives.

Be on the lookout for technical jargon and "corporate speak." Replace whenever possible, as appropriate to your audience. Examples:

Corporate Speak	People Speak
user, end user	people, staff, customers
new functionality	simplify, easier, cleaner
aging software	old system, outdated
user experience	how it feels
performance improvement	get things done faster, more effectively, more simply, more accurately
business is changing	rise to challenges, be competitive
data visibility	be able to see trends
corporate growth	job security, healthy company
communication	all on the same page, let us know, give a shout

Benefits of Simplicity

- Saves corporate investment in time, morale and dollars.
- People don't have to struggle with unnecessary terms.
- Teams can move forward with what they need to 'get the job done.'
- Prevents boredom, and the costs associated with boredom.

A TIMELINE for GETTING I.T. RIGHT:

Planning

Planning is critical. Note that proper planning constitutes approximately as much time as implementation, from 8 to 12 months.

Pre-planning	Planning A	Planning B	Planning C	Planning D	Action
Executive Choice to Add New System	Develop Executive Team Establish Cadence of Meetings	Develop Rationale, Metrics, and Preliminary Budget	Select Project Leader Establish Project Cadence and Reporting	Select Project Team Select Field Team Members	Due Diligence Select System and Vendors Including Consultant(s) Update and Finalize the Budget after Due Diligence
Communication	Communication	Communication	Communication	Communication	Communication
6 to 9 months	1 week	1 to 2 weeks	1 week	1 week	4 to 8 weeks

About the importance of Communication

As with all things in *Getting I.T. Right*, this timeline is a framework to provide readers with a sense of what must be done when installing the organizational "App." Your actual timeline may be different. The point here is that no system goes in flawlessly within just a few months. The upfront work is the key to the implementation. Effective communication—real-time updates for affected people, not just emails—is critical to success, yet often overlooked. Don't cut costs on communication!

The Ideal Enterprise App Introduction

Implementation
Generally 10 to 16 months are allowed for the action-taking part of the plan.

Training & GO LIVE
By these stages, 99% of the bugs should be worked out.

Action	KICK OFF	Pilot Run	Beta Test	Training	GO LIVE
Develop Communication Plan Develop Training Plan Get Field input through project Team Members	Announce to Field Conduct Process Analysis Write Technical Documents Code Database Cleanup and Transfer	Test Bug Fixes	Test Incorporate Feedback with Additional Fixes and Tweaks	Train trainers first and use short training sessions, max. 4 hours per class, to allow for absorption, processing, adaptation, and practice of the new way.	If all the preceding are done right, should be a smooth transition to the new way. Conduct Follow up Postmortem: Celebrate, Document What Worked, Capture Ideas for Future Improvements
Communication	Communication	Communication	Communication	Communication	Communication
4 to 8 weeks	6 to 9 months	1 month	1 month	1 to 2 weeks	1 day

Note that **Announcement** of the pending change to the field occurs during the Kick-Off stage, from 2 to 9 months ahead of the change.

Major Categories of Communications During an IT Change

Not everyone needs to know everything

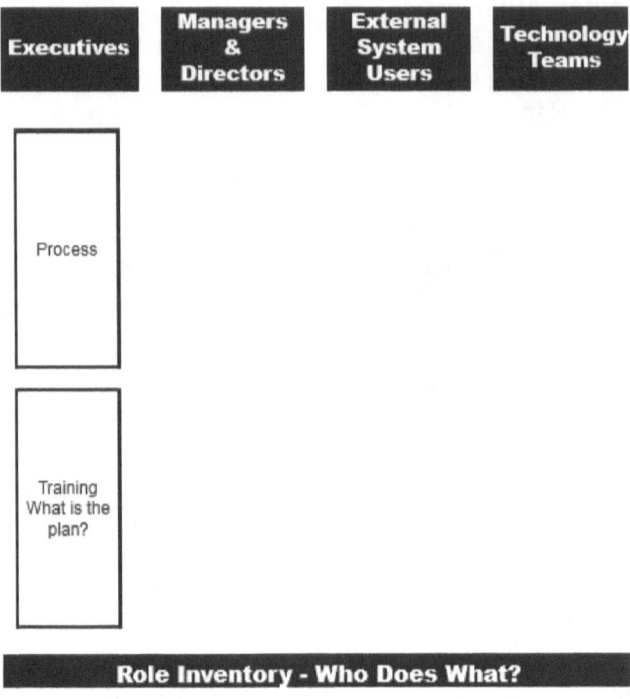

Figure 2. PROCESS CATEGORY

New processes are the heart and soul of application in a technology change. The reason the system is put in place is to do things differently. People who reengineer the processes and the people who are affected by the new processes need to know.

Once the new processes are put in place, a training plan is required for users. The training plan must be communicated effectively to executives, middle managers, and system users, especially those whose role has changed.

The ROLE INVENTORY simply means "Who is doing what in the new world?" In other words, if someone was formerly a customer service agent, but that role has been changed to a 'service agent', a precise clarification of that role is critical for effective service going forward. People need to know what they're doing!

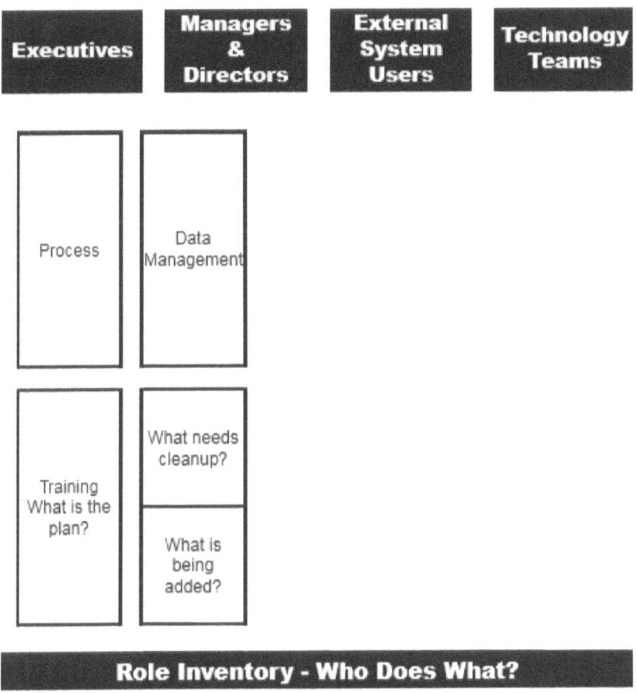

Figure 3. DATA CATEGORY

Data retrieval and analysis is flat out boring work requiring determination. Not everyone needs to know about data analysis, retrieval, and processing. But there are critical details that must be shared among people who are digging out the data. Run multiple conversions: Run - Test - Run - Test. Validation: is the conversion process working?

> Change management and effective communications is something that almost every client I've seen struggles and fails at. The **business should ensure that it is aligned with IT direction and vice versa, working together on a common goal** for the corporation's initiative and not having competing priorities.
>
> —Jason Juds, ERP consultant, Liberty Advisors, Chicago

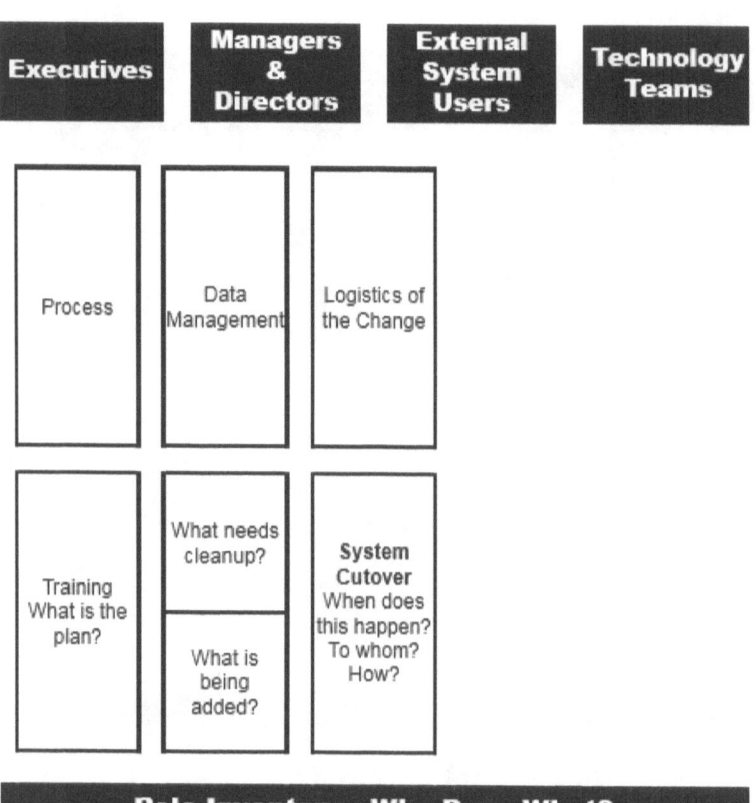

Figure 4. Logistics Category

GO LIVE logistics that many people in the organization should know. The details of what, who, where, and when are required for all parties in the change to ensure people know what is happening. This must be built into the Master Schedule.

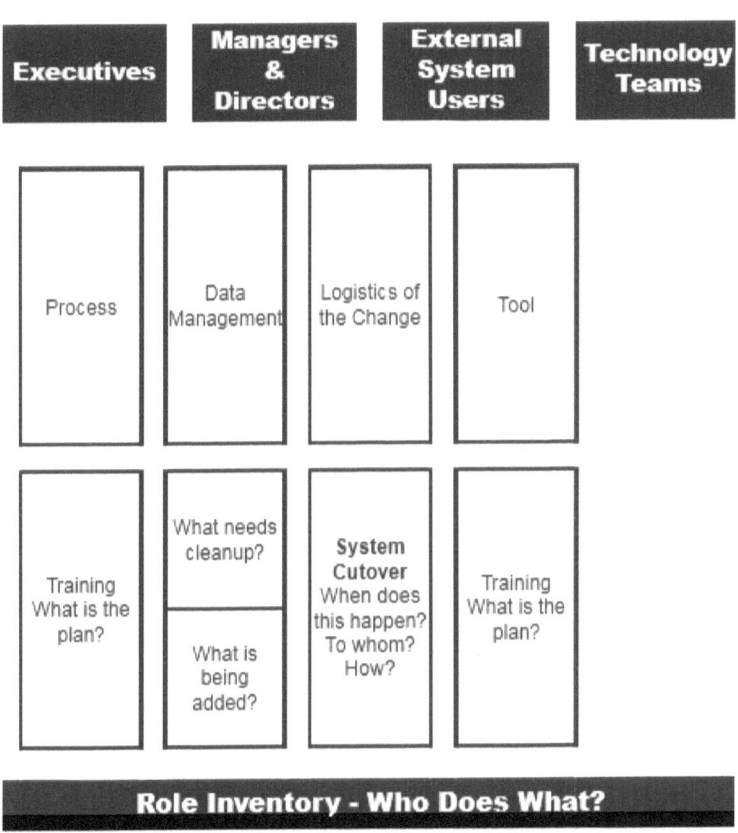

Figure 5. Training Category

Once the "Tool" (new system) is in place, a training schedule with details and trainers (discussed above) is a key component of communication.

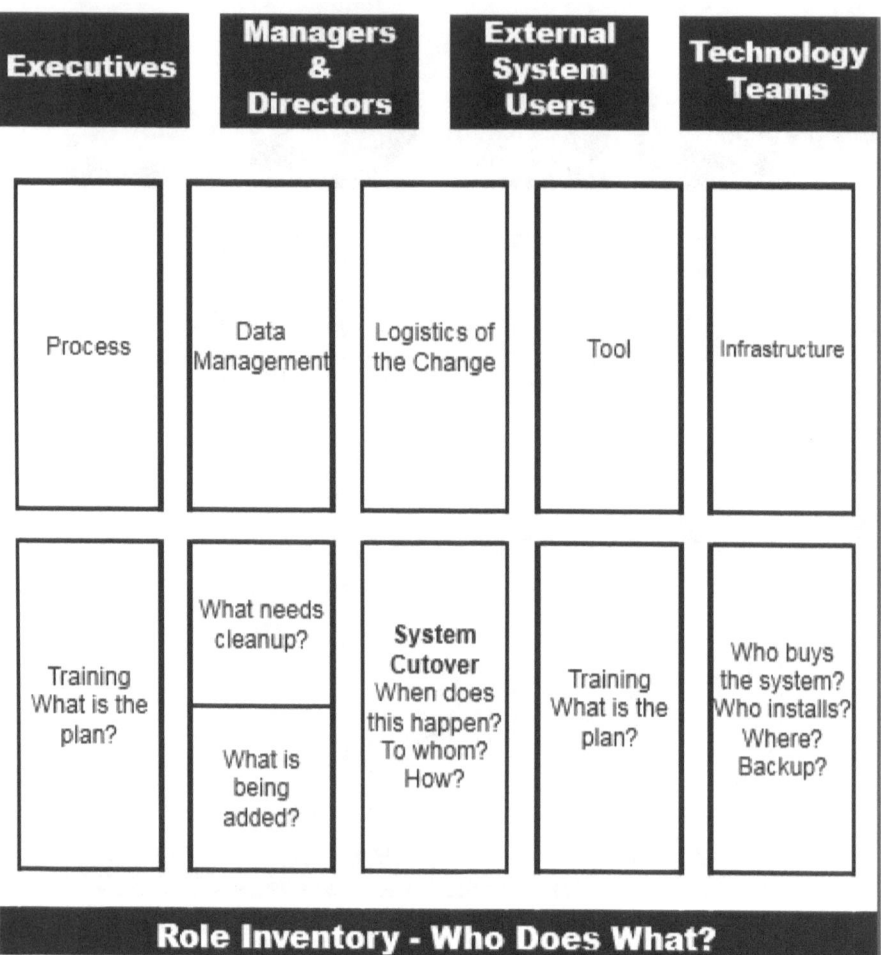

Figure 6. Infrastructure Category

This element of communication is often overlooked because it is a dull, boring element of technology change, yet it is critical to success because it provides the backbone of the system. Servers, the cloud, system interface, system support are all part of the infrastructure category of communication. Specialists in this domain must communicate lead times to project leadership and other technical team members. This information is NOT required to share with end users.

APPENDIX B – Terms

Big Fish, Small Pond Syndrome: Smaller organizations will be competing against larger organizations for support when challenging situations arise. Ensure your contract explains the terms of service, for example; "within 24 hours we will receive support from your technical team."

Change Management: The overall process of introducing a new system.

CRM: Customer Relationship Management. A system that tracks and manages customer inquiries, records of transactions, customer returns, sales history and so forth.

Distributed practice: (also known as spaced repetition or spaced practice): A learning strategy in which practice is broken up into a number of short sessions, over a longer period of time.

Due Diligence: 1) A measure of prudence, responsibility, and diligence that is expected from, and ordinarily exercised by, a reasonable and prudent person under the circumstances. 2) Duty of a firm's directors and officers to act prudently in evaluating associated risks in all transactions. 3) Duty of the investor to gather necessary information on actual or potential risks involved in an investment. 4) Duty of each party to a negotiation to confirm each other's expectations and understandings, and to independently verify the abilities of the other to fulfill the conditions and requirements of the agreement.

ERP: Enterprise Resource Planning, which includes production, finance, materials, inventory, and other core systems required for business management.

HRMS (or HRS): Human Resource Management System. A system that handles performance reviews, maintenance of employee records, time cards and so forth.

IoT: The Internet of Things. Connectivity between very dissimilar systems to share data and integrate actions. For example, the thermostat in your home is connected to your mobile phone.

LMS: Learning Management System. Repository for training records, training planning, scheduling and other learning services

Managing Change: Managing systems, revisions, and technical details.

Phasing communication: developing the right segments of content to be shared with the organization at different phases or points in time.

PMO: Project Management Office. A team of people who are experts in project management and provide resources in implementing major projects.

ROI: Return On Investment. ROI is usually expressed as a percentage and is typically used for financial decisions, to compare a company's profitability or to compare the efficiency of different investments. The return on investment formula is:

$$ROI = (Net\ Profit\ /\ Cost\ of\ Investment) \times 100$$

ROI Blindness: Unrealistic optimism that a project will generate a positive return on investment.

Role Inventory: Who is doing what in the new world; titles and job functions often change with new technology; understand and communicate these new functions in advance.

Scope: The extent of the area or subject matter that something deals with, or to which, it is relevant; part of project planning that involves determining and documenting a list of specific project goals, deliverables, tasks, costs and deadlines.

Scope Creep: What happens when additional goals, deliverables, and tasks get added to a project, increasing costs and extending deadlines.

Stressor: Any event, experience, or environmental stimulus that causes stress in an individual. These events or experiences are perceived as threats or challenges to the individual and can be either physical or psychological.

Structured interviews: A method of asking everyone the same questions to listen for common trends of issues. Everyone - from the executive suite to the frontline - get the same questions about the change. It is amazing the trends that come out!

APPENDIX C

Technical Articles

Included in this section are summaries of three articles worth reading in full and studying.

Bista Solutions identifies these top 10 reasons for ERP Implementation failures.

https://www.bistasolutions.com/resources/blogs/erp-implementation-failures/

1. Doing it in the first place.
2. No clear destination.
3. A good plan or just a plan?
4. Part-time project management.
5. Underestimating resources required.
6. Over-reliance on the consultants.
7. Customization.
8. On-the-job training.
9. Insufficient testing.
10. Not enough user training.

"The horror stories of failed ERP projects are now the stuff of legend. According to one recent report, more than 29% of ERP implementations fail to achieve even half the planned business benefits. Some well-known examples include Waste Management suing SAP for $500 million for a failed ERP implementation, Hershey Foods' 19% drop in profits from a failed SAP implementation at Halloween time a few years ago, the complete bankruptcy of FoxMeyer Drug, a $5 billion pharmaceutical distributor over a failed $100 million ERP implementation, and, perhaps most troubling, the over $1 billion spent by the US Navy on four different ERP systems, all of which have failed. There are many lessons to be learned from these failed ERP implementations."

CIO.com has published and continues to update a roundup of **the most "complex and expensive enterprise software market [failures]...packed with tales of vendor mud-slinging, outrageous hype...[and] plenty of drama,"** by Josh Fruhlinger and Thomas Wailgum.

> http://www.cio.com/article/2429865/enterprise-resource-planning/10-famous-erp-disasters--dustups-and-disappointments.html

---

Anupam Sharma at SAP elucidates **ERP implementation failures common mistakes**. While acknowledging "numerous challenges which can result in disastrous ERP Implementation," he focuses on what he sees as the two most common mistakes:

First, assuming an ERP project is just an IT project. "Everyone from the organisation should be involved in the transition journey," he says. Secondly, succumbing to the temptation to simply replicate legacy systems because it's easier than confronting resistance and unwillingness to embrace new ways. People must be helped to "think outside the box." That, he says, is a function of the quality of communication. And quality of communication is a function of leadership.

> https://blogs.sap.com/2013/10/03/erp-implementation-failures-common-mistakes/

APPENDIX D

Used by permission from Swick Technologies

This chart shows the complete technology installation of a new system.

Business Network Design & OSI

Open Systems Interconnect 7+1 Model

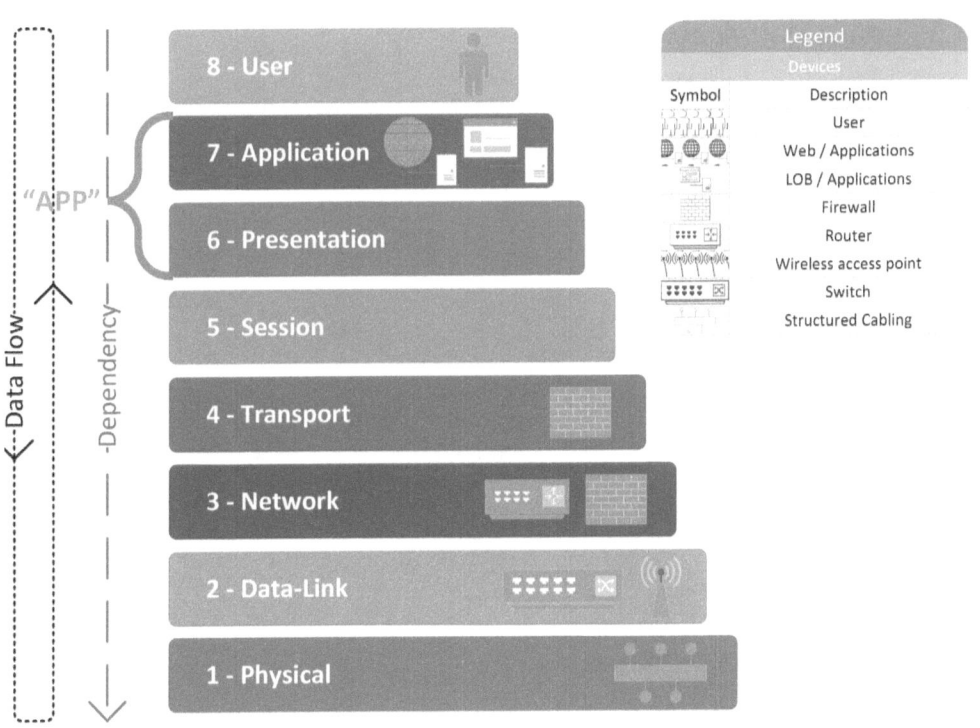

Notes / Bibliography

1. Towers Watson, *Only One-Quarter of Employers Are Sustaining Gains From Change Management Initiatives, Towers Watson Survey Finds*, Willis Towers Watson, 2013
   https://www.towerswatson.com/en/Press/2013/08/Only-One-Quarter-of-Employers-Are-Sustaining-Gains-From-Change-Management

2. Wall Street Journal, *Why digital transformations are hard.* 3/6/17 R14. CIO Network.
   https://www.wsj.com/articles/why-digital-transformations-are-hard-1488856200

3. Deloitte Consulting, *ERP's Second Wave: Maximizing the value of ERP-enabled processes*, 1998.
   http://www.ctiforum.com/technology/CRM/wp01/download/erp2w.pdf

4. Ibid, Towers Watson.

5. Robert Evans, *The human side of business process reengineering.* (Management Development Review. Vol. 7 (6). 10-12), 1994
   http://www.emeraldinsight.com/doi/abs/10.1108/09622519410074154

6. Snyder, Robert A. (2016) *The social-cognitive neuroscience of leading organizational change.* (New York: Routledge), 2016
   www.tandfebooks.com/doi/preview-pdf/10.4324/9781315707785

7. James Allen, N. Jimmieson, P. Bordia, & B. Irmer, B. *Uncertainty during organizational change: managing perceptions through communication.* (Journal of Change Management, 7:2; 187-210), 2007
   http://www.tandfonline.com/doi/abs/10.1080/14697010701563379

8. Susan A. Brown, Norman L. Chervany, & Bryan A. Reinecke, *What matters when introducing new information technology.* (Communications of the ACM. Volume 50 (9). 91-96), 2007
   http://dl.acm.org/citation.cfm?id=1284625

About the Author

Dr. Jim Bohn is "The Blue Collar Scholar." Raised by a factory-working father and armed with a PhD, Dr. Bohn puts proven theory on the table and invites you to roll up your sleeves and go to work. His organizational expertise, insight, and business savvy derives from decades of successfully leading leaders, observing, and evaluating the organizational behavior of multiple Fortune 500 organizations. Dr. Bohn's rare alloy of practice and theory is hard to find in today's market, making him a much-appreciated advisor.

A recognized expert on change, his book *Architects of Change: Practical Tools for Executives to Build, Lead and Sustain Organizational Initiatives*, has been endorsed by G.E., Walgreens, Lowe's, Comfort Systems USA, and others. Dr. Bohn's second book, *The Nuts and Bolts of Leadership*, was endorsed by Sodexo and the Water Council of Milwaukee.

In addition to his books and published research, teaching at the University of Wisconsin-Milwaukee, Concordia University, and Marquette University, and his work in organizational transformation, Dr. Bohn is a sought-after speaker at the *Milwaukee Business Journal* and the National Academy of Change Management Professionals. He's led workshops for SHRP and Wisconsin I/O Psychologists, ASTD-Twin Cities, MNCMN, MNODN, Atlanta Field Service Conference, Metro Milwaukee SHRM Annual Conference, SHRM SIGS, IFMA Twin Cities and the Chicago Corenet Real Estate Group among others, including PMI International, Minnesota PMI, the Volunteer Center of Ozaukee County, OFB, National Association of Credit Managers, The Neenah Police Department, the Plant Facilities Management Association, and PRSA along with multiple corporations across Southeast Wisconsin including Johnson Controls, Kohler and QPS.

Dr. Bohn served in a variety of roles in the corporate world beginning in 1973, personally leading the transformation of multiple underperforming teams to achieve award-winning levels of success. After several decades with a Fortune 100 company, he launched his own Change Management and Organizational Transformation Practice. Dr. Bohn has a unique blend of hands-on, in-the-trenches experience in addition to a rich pedigree of research from his doctoral studies. His research in Organizational Efficacy is groundbreaking and has been translated into Russian and Italian.

As a leader, Dr. Bohn has personally led significant change management projects. He has served in roles ranging from the shop floor to design, engineering, sales, and service. His customers include major hospital networks, manufacturing organizations, global legal teams, finance groups, and non-profits in projects ranging from leadership team development, mergers, organizational analysis, and large-scale change implementation including ERP projects across the US and in Europe. He has served as a Group Director for the Manufacturing Consortium Paranet Group.

Other Books by Jim Bohn, PhD

Architects of Change: Practical Tools to Build, Lead and Sustain Organizational Initiatives

The Nuts and Bolts of Leadership: Getting the Job Done

Fixing A Broken Team

Improving Managerial Effectiveness Through Proaction

The Art and Science of Middle Management

Available at **DrJimBohn.com** and book retailers.

Contact Jim Bohn, PhD

@DrJimBohn

info@proxios.com

DrJimBohn.com

Linkedin.com/in/jamesbohn/